SECOND EDITION

A Handbook for
Writing Formal Papers

FROM CONCEPT TO CONCLUSION

Norman W. Steinaker * Terry A. Bustillos

National University

Cover art: *Matisse Dream*, by George Herman

Printed in the United States of America

10 9 8 7 6 5 4 3 2 1

ISBN 0-536-16616-1

2005240496

MT

Please visit our web site at *www.pearsoncustom.com*

PEARSON CUSTOM PUBLISHING
75 Arlington Street, Suite 300, Boston, MA 02116
A Pearson Education Company

Table of Contents

2 space - apple #2

Preface

In the formal writing process you need to be organized, thoughtful, and clear. Formal writing is a pristine exercise in clarity, continuity, and cogent thinking. There are five words or steps which can illuminate this writing process. They are define, describe, detail, discuss, and determine. These steps are intrinsic to the process of writing and to the organization, clarity, and thoughtfulness of your paper. They are the sequential steps that writers of formal papers follow. In the formal writing process these five sequential steps are the key to writing a successful paper that brings understanding and meaning to the reader. You need to be continually cognizant of them as you write your paper. Remember also that formal writing, while it has a style and character of its own as well as a particular format, should also be lively and interesting to the reader. The careful sequencing of these five steps in the development of your paper, done with craft and skill, can infuse liveliness and interest into your work. Again, the five words are define, describe, detail, discuss, and determine.

Define. The first obligation you have to the reader is to define the topic of your paper. Definition consists of a clear, concise, and coherent characterization of the topic being studied. This should be done in the first few paragraphs of your paper, preferably in the first paragraph. Let the reader know immediately the subject and focus of the paper, so there is a clear understanding of the purpose and what is to come in the paper. In defining the paper you should indicate the limits and parameters of the paper. It is essential that this be done early in the paper so the reader can quickly and clearly comprehend the topic as well as its focus and limitations. If you are writing a research proposal or research study you need to define the questions or issues you are addressing and how you have approached them. Through the clear and careful exposition of the topic and issues in your paper, the reader can make a decision as to how the content could be used for personal or professional purposes. Definition is the equivalent of memory and

translation in the cognitive taxonomy and exposure in the experiential taxonomy (Steinaker &

Bell, 1979).

Describe. After the definition is clearly, concisely, and coherently stated, you will need

to describe the topic so the reader understands the focus of your paper. You will need to

provide, in the introduction or first section of your paper, some additional information to make it

clear to the reader how you have limited and focused the topic of your paper. You will also need

to establish the importance of the paper in the field. To do this you should provide the reader

with a few salient citations and specifics about the topic. The reader should not only know what

the topic is, but should have a clear understanding of why it is important. The reader should

know, through the specific information you have provided, the importance of the topic and how

it is to be focused and developed. You should also inform the reader why you have selected this

topic. All of these elements describe your paper and give it substance, meaning, and purpose.

When you have completed both the definition and the description, you have completed the

introduction or first section of your paper. This describing process corresponds to translation

and interpretation in the cognitive taxonomy and to participation in the experiential taxonomy.

Detail. In the review of literature and method sections of the paper you detail or tell

about what researchers, writers, and commentators have reported about the topic you have

selected and how you have organized your study. It is your task to detail and inform for the

reader, as objectively as possible, the information you have found through your reading and

reviewing the literature. You simply relate the information without personal comment and

without interpretation. You note, cite, and tell what has been done in the field and what you

have discovered through your own review of literature. Nothing more is needed and nothing more

should be done. You will need to organize your detailed information into categories and

subcategories in the review of literature to clarify it, to explicate it, and to structure your paper

for the reader. This kind of organization is always very helpful to the reader. You need to remember the review of literature provides the evidentiary basis for your discussion. When doing a research paper you will include a method section in which you detail the organization, the structure, and the process developed for your study. You will include information on data collection and analyses of these data. You must also include a results section in which you report your findings. These further add to your evidentiary base for your conclusions and recommendations. You may utilize existing research models or you may develop a model specific to your study. The detail step in writing corresponds to the application and analysis levels of the cognitive taxonomy and the identification level of the experiential taxonomy.

Discuss This step in the formal writing process is done, and logically so, in the discussion section of your paper. If you are doing a review of literature only, this will be the final section of your paper. If you are doing a qualitative or quantitative study, this section will follow the method and results sections and will be the concluding section of your study. In a research study you will discuss not only the review of literature, but also your method and findings from the study. For review of literature papers you first summarize what you have found in the literature you reviewed. Then you interpret the literature usually, but not necessarily, by category. The element you need to consider are as follows: You note consistencies and inconsistencies and you bridge the gaps. You compare and contrast. You construct and deconstruct. You identify the important and eliminate the non pertinent. You build your own perspective through this process. You let the reader know that you have understood, applied, and analyzed the information and the findings thoroughly and completely. Your discussion must be straight forward and professional. It must reflect the careful consideration you have given to the topic and the thoroughness of your review of literature. If you are doing an qualitative or quantitative study, this section follows the method and results

section. You not only review the literature, but you incorporate the review with your method and your findings and bring them together in the discussion section of your study. This process in your paper corresponds to the analysis and synthesis levels of the cognitive taxonomy and to the internalization level of the experiential taxonomy.

Determine In the final section of your paper you make determinations about the topic and what you have learned. Here you draw conclusions and make recommendations. These conclusions and recommendations should be consistent within the interpretation component of the discussion. They should reflect the summative evaluation of the literature you have reviewed, their correlation with the study, and the findings you have reported. These conclusions and recommendations should reflect the synthesis and evaluation levels of cognition. You should inform the reader why you have drawn your conclusions and why you have made your recommendations. The conclusions and recommendations should be stated clearly and succinctly. They are your final commentary on the topic and should summarize your thinking. Generate a succinct and strong statement of what you have thought, determined, concluded, and recommended in terms of the topic you have chosen and the study you have completed. Determining is consistent with the synthesis and evaluation levels of the cognitive taxonomy and the dissemination level of the experiential taxonomy.

Again, best wishes to you as you develop your paper. Make it important to you. Your readers will sense this and will react more positively to your work whether they agree with you or choose to disagree with you. Remember that your paper is a reflection of you and your professionalism. Make it the very best that it can be. In doing this you will have a product which will bring forth a sense of personal accomplishment.

In this course, as in many courses at your university or organization, you are expected to write a formal professional paper, a professional writing project, or a quantitative or qualitative

study. For some of you this may be your first experience in writing a paper of this kind. For others this may be a further experience in writing. For all, this will be an opportunity to demonstrate your skills in writing. Writing a formal paper is a challenging task, but can be done well if you begin early in the course or time frame, keep to a personal schedule, and follow the style and format adopted by your university or your organization.

This handbook has been prepared as a guide and a quick reference on how to organize your paper or your study. A section by section developmental format for writing your paper, and a notation of some of the expectations of style and format which you will follow in preparing your paper have been included. You need to remember that the style manual for your paper is the latest edition of the *Publication Manual of the American Psychological Association* (APA). Your paper will consist of the following sections: Title page, abstract, introduction, review of literature, method, results, discussion, and references. Appendixes and a bibliography, if you have them in your paper, will also be discussed. You should remember the method and results sections are included only for courses or papers requiring a quantitative or qualitative study. In some instances you may be asked to include a table of contents. The preparation of a table of contents is included as a part of this handbook in case it is expected or required.

If you are submitting a writing project, funding proposal, or any other kind of paper the format may vary somewhat even though the style may be consistent with the APA. Consult your instructor or your supervisor. Every professional graduate paper will contain each of the sections described in this guide except as noted above. Instructors or supervisors may make minor adjustments in organization, but the basic component sections of the paper will be prepared as outlined in this handbook. You need to remember every section of the paper begins at the top of a new page. These notes are organized so expectations for each section of the paper are discussed sequentially. Writing tips are included at the end of the notes for each

section of the paper. They are designed to help you focus on how to prepare the content of each section of your paper.

In the pages that follow, each section of the paper is discussed and described. There is a difference between a quantitative or qualitative study and a review of literature paper. Most papers written at the graduate level are reviews of literature. In only a few courses are papers requiring a research format expected. All elements of each section of formal papers and research studies are detailed in this work. Please be sure to refer to this work as you are writing your paper. You will be expected to adhere to the format and the writing style throughout your paper. In addition to the discussion on the sections of the paper, there are three additional components of this work that you will need to review carefully. The first component deals with common errors found in formal papers. If you study this when reviewing the preparation of the other sections of your work, you will be well on your way to writing a strong graduate paper or research study. The second component of this work is a commentary on formal writing conventions. This is provided to give you, as the writer, an additional perspective on writing formal papers. It is written in narrative form and provides another component and support for your writing. The third component is an end note with a focus on strategies for building your professional skills. Six appendixes are included. In Appendix A a checklists for writing each section of the paper both for review of literature papers and for research studies is included including table of contents and bibliography. It is important that you use these checklists because they provide a list of the expectations and requirements for each section of the paper or study. Page number referents for finding information about each items on the checklist are noted for each item within the checklist for that section of the paper. Appendix B has a suggested scoring rubric for formal papers. Appendix C is a suggested evaluation guide for formal papers. In Appendix D a format for presenting papers is provided. Appendix E contains a list of common

references. Appendix F is a guide to developing surveys and questionnaires. A glossary of terms

pertaining to writing and research is included following the appendixes.

There are many additional sources for writing papers and studies which can be used.

Among them are the *Publication Manual of the American Psychological Association* (American

Psychological Association, 2001), Cone and Foster's work (1993), Carver (1984), and Turabian

(1987). If you are in the field of education and need general resources, consult Darling-Hammond

(1997), Eisner (1994)), Joyce and Weil with Calhoun (2004), and Reeves (2003). If you need

additional resources in research use Gall, Borg, and Gall (1996), Mertens (2005), and Merriam

(1998). There are, of course, many more. If you are in the business department you may wish

to use, among others, Bennis (1997, 2000), Bennis and Goldsmith (2003), Drucker (1967),

Howard (1993), Sample (2003), or Likert (1967). Again, there are many more resources for you

to review and consult in these and other fields of study.

In this second edition a number of changes have been made. Additions and corrections

have be made in the explanations for how to do each section of the paper. These changes have

been more substantive in the method and results sections of the work. Writing tips have been

extended and are more detailed. There have been additions and changes made in the section on

common errors in formal papers. Additional information has been included in the section on

conventions of formal writing. In the sample references appendix, additional samples have been

included for writer's use. The glossary has been extended to include more terms students and

writers encounter in classes or in their organizations. We feel that, in this edition, the scope of

the work has been broadened and the content, while remaining user friendly, has been augmented

for clarity, specificity, and necessary detail. Many of the changes we have made have come to us

from students who have used the *Handbook* and from our colleagues. We thank them for helping

to make this edition one that writers will find even more useful than the first edition.

We wish to acknowledge the assistance and support of our colleagues, our friends, and our students for reading and critiquing this work. Their assistance and responses have been invaluable as we have prepared this document. In field tests and in reviewing the document our students have been very helpful in asking questions, helping us clarify meaning and content, and in critiquing the *Handbook* as they used it. Special thanks go to the late John W. Stallings of the University of Southern California for his support and guidance early in the development of this work. We also want to thank James Mbuva and. Lynne Anderson of National University for their review of the manuscript and for their support in making it better and more complete. We want to thank Marilyn Koeller and Lorraine Leavitt, our colleagues, for their encouragement and help. Especially, however, we want to thank our families. Their patience, their support and their love have meant much to us. Finally we want to thank the following: Dr. Natalia Bilan, Dr. Joseph R. Ruggio, and Dr. Richard A. Ott, without whom this work could not have been completed.

A Handbook For Writing Formal Papers:

From Concept to Conclusion

2nd Edition

Norman W. Steinaker

Terry A. Bustillos

National University

Abstract

The purpose of this work was to briefly explicate the format, organization, and style of formal papers for students. The *Publication Manual of the American Psychological Association* was the format adopted by many universities and organizations. This work was consistent with that manual. It was designed as a guide for students and others when writing formal papers. Five steps in writing a professional paper were included in the preface. Each section of the paper including title page, abstract, introduction, review of literature, method, results, discussion, references, and table of contents were addressed. Writing tips were included for each section. Conventions of formal writing were included. There were also discussions on common errors, and notes on building professional skills. Checklists for each section were included in an appendix.

Preparing the Title Page

The title page is the first page of the paper and contains the following elements: Page header, running head, title, author, and author's affiliation. Nothing more than this information needs to be included on the title page of the paper. This is what the American Psychological Association manual requires Be sure that the American Psychological Association (APA) style and format for this page are followed. If your professor, instructor, or supervisor has additional requirements, you should include them as part of your title page.

Page Header

The page header appears on the title page and every page of the paper including the abstract, reference section and appendixes. The page header consists of the first two words of the title of the paper and the sequential number of the page. The number and the second word of the page header are separated by a tab space of five to seven spaces. The page header is justified to the right margin. It is the only element of your paper that has a right margin justification. The page header is always located on the top right hand side of the paper on the first print line. The page header is how you number the pages of your paper. Do not use numbers at the bottom of the page or just the number at the top of the page. Each page of the paper including references, bibliography, and appendixes must have a page header with the page numbers in sequential order. The title page is page one of the paper. The rationale for this is that the pages are submitted and read by the reviewer in loose leaf order. If there is a mixup of the pages, the page header serves to help reorder the pages.

Running Head

The running head is placed on the title page one double space below the page header and is justified to the left margin. The r in running head is capitalized. The h in head is not capitalized. The words running head are followed by a colon. Following the colon, is the running

head which is simply a short version of your full title. All letters in all words of the running head are in capital letters. There is a specific purpose for the running head. You are writing a professional paper that is suitable for publication. The running head you have selected tells the reviewer and the editor what you would like to use as the header for each page of your article or paper when it is published. This is also how your paper will be referred to in professional discussions and in some bibliographies and abstracts. The running head appears only on the title page of your paper.

Title

The full title of your paper is centered mid page. The first letter of each word of the title is capitalized except for articles. If the title is lengthy, it should be divided appropriately into two lines with the second line being justified and centered under the first line. Do not use acronyms in your title. Write out the acronym. Do not use italics, abbreviations, or quotations marks in your title. Your title is a descriptor of your paper or study. Make it clear and concise.

Author

One double space below the title is your name. Your name is centered and justified with the title. Do not use the word by. For two authors, separate the names of the authors with the word and. Names should be placed on one line, space permitting. For three or more authors separate the names by a comma. Before the last author is listed use the word and. Authors names, if necessary, can be placed on two or more lines with the names centered and justified under the title.

Author's Affiliation

This is the university affiliation or professional affiliation of the author. In most cases the affiliation will be the university in which you are enrolled or the organization of which you are a member. If you are submitting this paper for publication you may use the university, your

school district, or your professional affiliation. The affiliation notation is centered one double space below the author's name. No other information appears on the title page. Do not put date, course title, course number, instructor's name, or any other information on the title page unless required by the professor, the instructor, or your supervisor.

Writing Tips

Be sure to follow the format explicitly. The title page is the first page the reader sees. It should reflect the information needed. The page header must be justified on the right margin at the top of the page. Ensure that the title, your name, and your affiliation are centered at mid page. Count the spaces if necessary. Select the running head carefully; it is a shorter version of your title. The running head is justified on the left. Do not use acronyms, italics, abbreviations, or quotation marks in the title or in the running head. Remember that the running head is written with all capital letters and is one double space below the page header. Make the title of your paper clear, cogent, and concise.

For a quick review of all the required components of the title page refer to the checklist for the title page in Appendix A on page 71. The use of this checklist will ensure that you have included all the necessary components of the title page in your paper.

Preparing the Table of Contents

A table of contents is not included in most formal papers because they tend to be relatively short. For longer papers and manuscripts such as this *Handbook*, a table of contents can be very helpful. A table of contents may also be required by your instructor or supervisor. Tables of content are included immediately following the title page. Tables of colntents are numbered in lower case Roman numerals as is the preface if one is included. Roman numerals are used only for the table of contents and any preface or prefatory remarks.

Lower case Roman numerals, as noted, are used in the table of contents and are numbered on the same line as the page header one tab space from the last letter of the page header. The page header is justified to the right margin. The title of the section, table of contents, is centered one double space below the page header. The name of each section or chapter of the work is entered on a line beginning one double space below the table of contents title. A dotted line with one space between each dot completes the line to the page number which is justified on the right. Each suceeding section is listed one double space below the preceding section When categories are included, they must be indented one tab space on the line below the section title. There must be at least two categories when they are listed. This pattern continues until all sections and categories are noted by page numbers. Page numbers are provided for each section, category, and subcategory. The page numbers are justified on the right margin. If your paper has subcategories, they are indented two tab spaces from the left margin or one tab space more than categories. If you have subcategories in your table of contents there must be at least two. See the table of contents for this document as an example of how to prepare your table of contents.

Writing Tips

Preparing a table of contents must be done accurately and carefully. Be sure that you have one space between each dot on the line from the end of the title of that section, category, or

subcategory to the number of the page. Remember that page numbers are justified on the right. Use Arabic numbers only, except for the notation of the preface. Categories are indented one tab space and are entered on the line below the section or chapter title. There must be at least two category titles when they are used. If you have subcategories, they are indented and entered two double spaces from the left margin or one tab space more than categories. There must be at least two subcatgory titles entered when they are used. Just a word on prefaces and prefatory remarks. Prefaces are not included in short papers or research studies and if they are, they serve to introduce the work, to illustrate its organization, and to acknowledge those who assisted you and supported you during the development of the work. Do not include any prefatory comments unless specifically asked to do so by your instructor or supervisor.

For a quick review of the expected elements of the table of contents, refer to the checklist in Appendix A page 72. The use of this checklist will help ensure that you have completed the required components of the table of contents.

Preparing the Abstract

The abstract is page two of your paper. An abstract, as a model, is included on page two

of this work. The abstract has a page header numbered as page two of the paper. Below the

page header is the word abstract which is centered one double space below the page header. The

a in abstract is capitalized, none of the other letters in the word is capitalized. The purpose of

the abstract is to inform the reader very succinctly about the purpose of the paper, the

parameters of the topic included in the paper, and the pertinence or importance of the paper in

the field. You should also note salient points you have found in your review of literature. If you

have written a research study you will state the problem or question you investigated as part or

all of the purpose of the paper. Your findings, conclusions, and recommendations are also

included. Readers will choose to read your paper or not to read your paper based on what you

include in the abstract. The abstract thus becomes the most important part of your paper in

terms of how many people read your paper. It must be very carefully written.

The APA limits the abstract to no more than 960 characters or about 120 words. In some

instances instructors or supervisors may allow you up to 150 words. Readers are interested in a

quick overview of your paper. Any additional words could deter from the purpose of the

abstract which is to inform reviewers and readers and to cause them to be interested in your

work. In order to conserve words use no citations and be as succinct as possible. At the same

time, however, be very specific about the content, conclusions, and recommendations of your

paper.

The abstract is not indented. It is blocked. It consists of one paragraph with all lines

justified only on the left margin of the paper. Right margins are not justified in the abstract, nor

are they justified on the right margin anywhere in the paper except for the page header and the

page numbers in the table of contents. The narrative of the paragraph begins one double space

below the word abstract. All narrative lines are double spaced. Do not break words at the end of

a line. No line should end with a hyphen. A good abstract is accurate, concise, and specific. You

report what the paper was about and include in the abstract salient points from your review of

literature, your findings, your conclusions, and your recommendations. The abstract is not

evaluative. No personal opinions or statements can or should be included. The conclusions and

recommendations which should be included in the abstract are the nearest you can come to

expressing your ideas or perspectives and even these should retain a non evaluative tenor.

Abstracts are written in the past or present perfect tense. The opening sentences define

the purpose of the paper or the issues studied in your paper. These sentences identify the

parameters and limitations of the paper and its importance to the field. The next few sentences

emphasize the major points from the review of literature as well as notations on your method and

your findings if you have done a research study. In the last few sentences of the abstract

summarize your conclusions and recommendations.

The abstract is the last section of the paper that is written. You usually complete the

introduction, review of literature, the method, the results, and the discussion sections before

writing the abstract. Once you have completed the paper and understand clearly the scope,

sequence, and findings of your work, you can then write the abstract with more clarity,

precision, and focus. Write clearly and concisely using simple sentences so that the reader can

quickly gain insight into the topic of your paper, its purpose, its parameters, what you learned

about the topic, your findings, and your conclusions and recommendations. Avoid citations in

the abstract because they count as words and thus decrease the number of words you can use to

tell the reader what needs to be understood about the paper.

When your paper has been published the abstract may appear as the initial introduction

or paragraph of your paper in the journal of publication. It may or may not be noted as the

abstract. Abstracts are also published in various professional publications such as Educational Resources Information Center (ERIC) and APA Psychological Abstracts.

Writing Tips

Be sure to keep to the word limitation of 120 to 150 words. Your abstract is written in the past or present perfect tense. Eliminate any unnecessary words or phrases. Use short simple sentences as much as possible. Do not use acronyms in the abstract. Avoid using adjectives and adverbs as much as possible. Use technical terms and language only if they are absolutely necessary. Do not include citations. Remember to include conclusions and recommendations. These are generally included in the last sentence or sentences of the abstract. In a research study you should include the question or issue you studied. You need to note whether it was a quantitative or qualitative study or a combinations of both major kinds of studies. You will also need to include a summary statement of the findings or the results of your study.

For a quick review of the expected elements of the abstract refer to the checklist for abstracts in Appendix A on page 73. The use of this checklist will help ensure that you have included all expected components of the abstract in your paper.

Preparing the Introduction

The introduction is the first narrative section of your paper. It is noted on the page header as page three of your paper. You center the full title of your paper one double space below the page header. If you need two lines for the title of your paper use them. Be sure the second line of the title is centered one double space below the first line of the title. All first letters in the words of the title are capitalized except for articles. Do not title this section introduction.

In the introduction there are three basic components. First, you define the purpose of the paper. If you are writing a research study you need to include in your purpose the question or issue you are studying. Second, you establish the importance of the topic in the field of study. Third, you provide a rationale for choosing the topic and for your interest in the topic. Nothing more is necessary for inclusion in the introduction.

Purpose of Paper

In defining the purpose of your paper you provide only as much information as is necessary. The purpose or purposes can be written in a few sentences or, depending on the topic, can be slightly longer. Make sure the reader has a clear understanding of the purpose of the paper; how you have defined it, and its limitations. If your problem or topic has many components or facets you will need to define the parameters of your paper carefully and make sure that the focus is clearly stated and specific. You may also include the issue or question being reviewed or studied. The reader needs to understand the purpose at the beginning of the paper. Make your purpose clear and provide as much information as you need to provide the reader with a clear and concise presentation of your purpose in writing the paper.

If you are preparing a quantitative or qualitative study, you will need to clearly define the question or the issue and the variables being studied in the purpose of your paper. You may also

need to include some information on population and process as well as on data collection instruments and how they were evaluated. This information must be briefly stated and provide enough information for the reader to clearly understand the focus, limitations, and parameters of the study. In writing your statement of purpose, you need to make it concise, clear, and cogent and provide as much information you feel the reader needs. In many instances you are writing within a specified time frame or deadline so your topic or purpose must be something you can develop well within the time frame under which you are working. Your first paragraph or few paragraphs of the introduction should make the purpose of the paper clear to the reader and provide the reader with a focused purpose for the paper as well as its parameters and limitations.

Importance of Topic

After you have written your purpose statement, you have the obligation to emphasize the importance of the topic. Remember that the work you are preparing is a professional paper or research study and needs to evidence a substantive contribution to the field. In this component of the introduction you will briefly bring forward issues that will be reviewed in your paper and develop a background for the reader so that the topic and the issues within it are recognized as important to the profession. This background of information should be defined and prepared with clarity and with evidence to support it. You should discuss briefly the literature you have reviewed and cite only salient points from your review. You do not go into great detail in the introduction because you will do this in your review of literature. In the introduction you are defining and describing, not going into detail. Your review of literature will be organized around categories and subcategories of your topic. You may want to organize this part of the introduction around those categories, though this is not mandatory nor is it essential in establishing the importance of the topic. You will need to use some citations in this section, but do not go into an exhaustive review of literature. As the writer you cannot establish the

importance of the topic. The importance is established only by the sources , authors, and researchers you cite Touch only on the pertinent and seminal sources that emphasize the importance of topic, the question, or the issues. Do only enough so that the reader understands the importance of the topic and has a good grasp of the background of the topic as well as the limitations and parameters of the paper. The reader should know not only the subject of the paper and its importance, but also know the specific issues and topics that are the focus of your paper as well as some of the resources you discuss within the review of literature.

Rationale for Choosing Topic

To provide closure in the introduction you will want to identify the rationale or your reason for selecting this topic. Let the reader know why you are doing the paper or the study and why you have an interest in the issues or questions discussed in your paper. Your choice can come from a personal need to learn more about the topic. It can come from a feeling that exploring the area and studying it will help you become professionally more competent. Your choice can also be made because this topic has within it issues that are pertinent in your school district or workplace. The rationale for a research study could be the need to test a theory, an intervention, or to determine attitudes and perspectives about an issue or problem. There could also be other professional reasons. You define your reasons and state them succinctly and to the point. Do not go into great detail.

Writing Tips

It is important to remember to write the introduction in a non evaluative style. You do not reveal any biases, predetermined expectations, or outcomes at this point in the paper. Your writing should reflect your professional interest in the topic and a recognition that it is important to you and to the profession. Everything in this section is written in the past tense or present perfect tense except for direct quotes. This is very important and you should review what you

have written to correct any tense as well as other syntactic issues. One of the most common errors for those who are just beginning the process of writing formal papers is syntax. Avoid compound and complex sentences as much as possible though they may occasionally be necessary. Write clearly and use short simple sentences consistently to ensure clarity and continuity. Say only what needs to be said and use an economy of expression. Keep in mind that "brevity is the soul of wit." Pope was correct. You can write with clarity, cogency, and develop continuity through saying only what needs to be said briefly and still retain interest and involvement by the reader. Your reader should understand the purpose of the paper, why it is important, and why you have an interest in the topic. This is most important and you must ensure that these are included in the paper. Sometimes writers include a transitional paragraph after the three components have been finished. While this is not necessary, it can give the reader an understanding of what is coming next in the paper and how the remaining sections are organized. This paragraph, if it is included, is generally brief, but may help the reader make a smooth transition from the introduction to the review of literature and a clear picture of how you have organized the paper. Finally, do not use superscript or subscript in your paper unless it is a scientific or mathematical formula or is approved for usage by the APA.

For a quick review of the expected elements of the introduction refer to the checklist for the introduction in Appendix A on page 74. The use of this checklist will help you ensure that you have included all the necessary components of the introduction in your paper.

Preparing the Review of Literature

The section of your paper following the introduction is called the review of literature.

This section is a major professional component of your paper. It also provides the foundation

for information and commentary about your topic. It is titled review of literature. The review of

literature begins on a separate page with the title centered one double space below the page

header. The review of literature is almost always the longest and most detailed section of your

paper and informs the reader about the literature you have reviewed. It provides your report on

the issues and content of the literature reviewed. The review of literature includes only sources

which are pertinent to your paper. Your review of literature also provides an evidentiary base

for your conclusions and recommendations. If you are writing a quantitative or qualitative

research paper the review of literature not only provides an evidentiary base for the question or

issue you are studying or testing, but in addition, provides the reader with a review of concurrent

and corollary research in the field. The review of literature is generally organized with an

introductory paragraph, categories delineating major areas of focus within the review, and

sometimes with subcategories within the broader categories. The introductory paragraph serves

as an organizational content design for your paper and should be brief and clearly written. In

some instances a closing paragraph may be included, even though it is not generally necessary in

most papers.

Introductory Paragraph

The introductory paragraph of the review of literature is generally relatively brief and

contains only information about how the review of literature is organized. You will name the

categories in the sequence in which they appear in the review. Names of categories and

subcategories are not capitalized unless they are proper nouns or are the first word following a

colon. If you include categories that have subcategories, you will name the subcategories

immediately following the naming of the category. Subcategories are necessary when they help you focus on specific information within a larger category. There must be at least two categories within the paper. Likewise, there must be at least two subcategories within each category where they are used. The names of the categories should be brief; usually one or two words and seldom more than three or four words. In a qualitative or quantitative study, you will follow the same content guidelines for your introductory paragraph. The categories should relate directly to research in the area of study as well as related categories pertinent to your study. Do not provide any other information in the introductory paragraph. The purpose of the paragraph is only to inform the reader about the organization of the review of literature. Immediately following the opening paragraph, the title of the first category is provided. The title of each category is on a separate line and is in italics.

Categories

A category in your review of literature helps you organize your review into logical areas of focus and that are defined areas of emphasis. Using categories helps the writer organize findings and information for the review in terms of identified components of the paper as noted in the purpose of the paper and stated in the introduction. Categories also help the reader to focus on specific information related to the content of the category. Each category needs to relate to the purpose of the paper or study as you have defined it in the introduction. The name of each category is on a separate line and is written in italics one double space below the narrative line above. Every word in the category is capitalized except for articles. The name of the category is justified on the left margin. The narrative begins on the next line.

When writing about your findings, you must be objective. No personal opinions, biases, or interpretations can be expressed in the review of literature. Avoid value words when writing the review. Let the researchers, the authors, and commentators speak for themselves. You can

paraphrase their works and use direct quotes, but you do not comment on them. Your comments are reserved for the interpretation component of the discussion section of your paper. You should write the review of literature in the past tense or the present perfect tense with the exception of direct quotes where the author may use the present or future tense. Remember every resource you have reviewed has already been written and published in some context. If there are differing views among the researchers or writers within a particular category you should indicate this, but without personal comment or interpretation. Direct quotes require citations and page numbers. Quotes of forty or more words must be blocked. To block a quotation indent every line of the quotation one tab space and do not use quotation marks. All blocked quotes are double spaced. If you paraphrase a researcher's or author's work, you must provide a citation. Indeed, every time you bring new information to the attention of the reader there must be a citation. Every paragraph including new information must have one or more citations. You must follow APA style and format for all citations.

You should go into as much detail as necessary when you are reviewing an article, a book, a document, internet material, visual material, or other resource. Through the material you have reviewed you are presenting information about the topic for the reader and providing an evidentiary basis for your interpretation, findings, conclusions, and recommendations. These become part of the discussion section of the paper. You are also demonstrating the importance of your sources in the field and their relationship to the paper or to the study. Furthermore, you need to provide for the reader a clear understanding of how the resource related to the category in which it is cited, to the topic, and to what the authors presented or found in their articles, books, or studies. It is important that the citation be consistent in content with the context of the category and the topic. In the review of literature you provide the reader with the information you have determined to be pertinent in explicating the issues, questions, or problems you have

defined as the focus and purpose of your paper or study.

Subcategories

Subcategories are component parts of a category. You must have at least two subcategories in each category to justify their use. Subcategories provide for more specific areas of focus or component parts of the category in which they appear. You have more organizational flexibility when you use subcategories. For example, if your category is teaching strategies, in each subcategory you can focus on one of the identified strategies chosen for review. Subcategories follow the same organization and writing style as categories. Titles of subcategories should be no more than two or three words. The title of each subcategory is written in italics. It is indented one tab space and is followed by a period. The narrative begins immediately following the title of the subcategory on the same line as the title of the subcategory.

Closing Paragraph

A closing paragraph is infrequently included, but if your review is lengthy or you wish to recapitulate the organization, you can include this paragraph. The only purpose of this paragraph is to again remind the reader what you have done in the review of literature. You simply rename the categories and subcategories to remind the reader what you have included in your review of literature. You do not introduce new information or use citations. You write your closing paragraph without personal commentary or interpretation. That is reserved for the discussion section of the paper. In most instances this paragraph is not needed, but if you feel the need to include it, please do so.

Writing Tips

The review of literature is usually the longest section of your paper. It is written in narrative form and must follow the APA format and style. Clarity of expression and logical continuity are important elements of writing. Use an economy of expression. Say only what

needs to be said. Use simple sentences most of the time. Compound and complex sentences should be avoided, unless needed for explanation or clarification. Avoid the use of jargon, buzz words, and overuse of professional terminology. Do not use colloquialisms, idioms, or slang expressions in your paper. You are writing a formal paper. You are writing for an audience of your peers and they read the paper with similar professional backgrounds and experiences.

Your review of literature should be written in the past or present perfect tense except for direct quotes. Whenever you introduce new information to the reader, you must cite the source of that information. If you use a direct quote, you must cite the source and the page number. Use quotation marks at the beginning and end of direct quotes of less than forty words. Direct quotes of forty or more words must be blocked. You do not use quotation marks with blocked quotes. If a blocked quote has a quotation within it, use an apostrophe to show that quotation. Do not use superscript or subscript except in certain mathematical or scientific formulae as defined within the APA *Manual*.

You should predominantly use the active voice in your writing. Be very careful to eliminate any anthropomorphisms. Remember that research cannot tell or report, neither can articles or books say. Only researchers and authors can tell, report, write, or say. Even in this day of political correctness, there should be agreement of subject and verb as well as in personal pronouns. Avoid the use of he/she even though in a very few cases it may be unavoidable. Sentences, if they are well crafted, can for the most part, be written without using he/she. Make sure the reader understands the referent when you use a personal pronoun. When referring to people use who or whom. When referring to animals or inanimate objects use that. While there are certain well defined conventions for formal writing, they must be followed. At the same time you should strive to make your paper lively and interesting to the reader. Simplicity and continuity creates a more fluent paper where meaning is more easily understood. You can go into

as much detail as is necessary through a simple, straightforward, cogent style. Strive to make

your review of literature reflect this kind of narrative flow. Be sure also to edit and carefully

review this section of your paper or study. This is important in order to make sure that your

review of literature is consistent with the purpose of your paper. Your review of literature

provides an evidentiary base for your conclusions and recommendations. The review of literature

should also reflect the content necessary to ensure that the reader clearly understands the scope

and sequence of the resources you have reviewed and how they pertain to your topic. Be sure

that everything in the review of literature is double spaced.

For a review of the elements necessary to the review of literature refer to the checklist for

the review of literature in Appendix A on page 75. The use of the checklist will ensure that you

have included all the components of a review of literature in your paper.

Preparing the Method Section

A method section is included only in papers when you are doing a qualitative or quantitative research study. In a research study the method section immediately follows the review of literature. Almost all other formal papers are referred to as review of literature papers. Some graduate classes require a research study. If you are doing a research study and need to include a method section you must to include the following categories: Question or issue being studied, limitations of the study, variables, population, sample size, time frame, process, data collection, data analysis, and assessment and evaluation. In some instances there may be some redundancy, but in each category there is a defined focus with the need to present the information from a specific perspective. Research studies can be either quantitative or qualitative.

Quantitative studies are experimental, empirical, and statistical. The focus is on prediction, attitudes and perceptions, confirmation, and testing interventions or hypotheses. The analysis is deductive and the findings are precise and numerical. Qualitative studies focus on the nature and essence of groups. They involve case studies, fieldwork, ethnography, and phenomenology. The goal of a qualitative investigation is understanding the beliefs and attitudes of a group, the structure of identified phenomena, constructivist methodology, and generating grounded theory. The mode of analysis is inductive and the findings are comprehensive and richly descriptive. You need to determine which of these approaches to research would be more appropriate for your study. In some instances a study could include both kinds of research approaches. Each of the categories in a research study is given below with a brief description of the content that should be included in each category. The title of each category is italicized and on a separate line from the text as shown below.

Question or Issue

The questions or issues you are studying are the core purposes of your paper. You stated them as part of the purpose in the introduction to your paper and you need to restate them at the very beginning of your method section. In this section of the paper you need to clarify for the reader the issues and questions motivating the study as well as specific variables being tested. You delimit the area of study within the identified questions or issues noted. You need to be very specific here so that the reader clearly understands what you are studying and how you have focused your particular study. These initial statements of the question or issue are key to the method section of your paper and need to be very carefully done. In this category of the method section you are delimiting the scope of the paper and defining its parameters. Craft it so there is no ambiguity about what your questions or issues are and how you are framing them. You also need to note the specific focus of the study. You are stating the purpose of the research, the questions or issues studied, and the variables tested. You are also defining as the limitations of the study. You may need also to include briefly some information on the population, measures used, process, and analyses of the date even though these will be more fully developed later. Here they simply provide a very brief overview of the study and are included for clarity of understanding about the study.

Limitations

There has never been a study that is totally complete and without flaw. Every research study has limitations and defined parameters. You need to point out some of those limitations in the study you are doing. Among those limitations could be the size of the population and whether they volunteered, were a convenience sample, or were selected at random. Limitations could also be areas of information or the variables that you are studying or that you are not studying. Limitations can be the time frame for completing the study. Limitations help the reader understand what you are not including in the study and what the constraints of the study

imply for your work. Limitations can also be resources, funds, and materials available. Limitations could further include the kind of instruments selected for gathering and analyzing data. Other limitations could include variables studied, resources, and personnel. In this section you need to make clear to the reader how each of these limitations affected the study or related to the outcomes.

Variables

In any research paper there are many variables that could be studied. The demographic data in a survey, questionnaire, or interview can help you identify the variables. An intervention or a treatment to a group can constitute a variable. In this category of the method section you list the variables you plan to test in the study. You may also note some you are not testing. Variable definition is exceptionally important both to you and to your readers. Each component element you are testing or studying can be a variable. You need to know and your readers need to know very specifically and definitionally the variables which you are testing within the study. The definition of variables provides for the reader a clear statement of what you are studying or what you are testing. Some research studies fail because the variables tested are not clearly defined. Variables should have a direct relationship to the purpose of the study. Sometimes you may be working with only one variable, but often two or more variables are involved in the study. You may want to focus on the expected outcomes for the variables and interpret them for their impact on the population. If you do this they need to be noted with details and interpretation in the results and discussion sections of the study. You can also note related variables not included in the study. You need to include all these items in the variable category of your method section.

Population

Who you are studying is also very important. You identify the population studied in this category of the method section. Populations vary in terms of the kind of study in which you are

involved. Quantitative studies usually, but not always, require both a control and experimental group. These two groups need to be as equally matched as possible. Quantitative studies can also include a population responding to surveys, questionnaires, or interviews. Qualitative studies generally require only one group. Population size can vary according to the nature of the study. If you are doing a single case study your population is one person. If you are doing a large quantitative study your population could be hundreds or even thousands. If you are doing a lengthy or longitudinal study, you need to account for an attrition of members of the identified population. You must define age group, characteristics, gender, commonalities, and differences. You need to provide the reader information on how you selected the population and why they were selected. Note whether they were selected randomly or were a convenience population. Note any criteria used for selection of the population. These criteria could be experience, achievement, specific skills, or other identified personality or behavioral attributes. Do this notation clearly and succinctly for your readers. Make sure they clearly understand how the population was selected, why it was selected, and the criteria used for their selection. It is important for your readers to know this if they wish to replicate the study.

Sampling Process

This could be a separate category in the method section of your study, or it could be included within the population category subsection. You may break this out as a separate section if you need to describe in detail your sampling strategies and procedures. Here, you need to provide a rationale for the size of the population, how the population is selected, and why it is limited to the particular size you chose. You may need to justify the size of the population in terms of why it is not larger or smaller. Sample size information could also include details about any subgroups within the population and how they might relate to variables being tested. You may also need to note the kind of sampling techniques used in selecting your population. You

may, for example, need to note variances in achievement, experience, or skills as being subgroups in the population. The use of sample size as a separate subcategory in the method section of the paper allows you to do a more detailed description of the nature of the population in terms of subgroups within it and in terms of variables tested. You need to note how you chose your sample. Note whether it was a random selection or a convenience sample. Other sampling strategies used also need to be addressed in this category. This kind of information could also help frame the selection and definition of the variables studied.

Time Frame

Here you simply provide the reader with the time frame for the study. Within this time frame you may want to note the sequence of activities and events in the study such as pre and post tests, as well as points of emphasis and benchmarks at specific times during the study. The category on the time frame can include information such as when and how data are collected, when data is analyzed, and when the final report of the study will be ready. A time frame is not only the beginning time and ending time, it is a catalogue and sequence of activities and events within the time frame. The time frame will help keep you on task and oriented toward an appropriate sequence of activities within the time frame. It will also keep the reader informed about the time sequence in which the study was done and the activities and events involved therein. If the reader wishes to replicate the study, the specifics of the time frame can be very helpful.

Process

In this category of the method section you tell the reader how you did the study. In a quantitative study you note the pre and posttests and the nature of the intervention or treatment. In a qualitative study you note your observations, interviews and and review of documents. You indicate how you coded the data from them. For both kinds of research study you explain the

process in a step by step sequential manner. You need to be careful to note each of the sequential steps and discuss each step briefly. If you have problems with any step in the process, be sure to mention them. Your purpose in this part of the method section is to delineate the formative process and make it clear to the reader. In effect, this is a brief overview of the study and how it was accomplished. This category of the method section can also include brief statements about how the data was gathered, analyzed, and evaluated. A more explicit discussion of these topics comes later in the method section, but for the reader to understand the process, you will want to briefly note them. In any study there are formative processes and summative processes. The formative process is as important as the summative findings of the study if the study is to be replicated or the findings implemented. In this category of the method section you focus on the formative process. You need to relate the formative process with the summative outcomes briefly in this category of the method section of the paper. When the reader finishes this part of the paper, there should be a clear understanding of how you completed the study, the steps within the process and the linkage of that process to the summative outcomes.

Data Collection

How you collect the data is essential information for the reader. You need to include, in this category, information on the instruments you used in your study. You need to tell about the tests, questionnaires, observations, surveys, interviews, document reviews, and any other measures you used to gather data on your population and on the variables tested. Instruments and other measures used need to be described and made clear to the reader. These measures will be different in qualitative and quantitative studies. In qualitative studies the researcher is the primary instrument. You generally use interviews, observations, and document reviews including historical documents. You need to explain how you coded the responses in terms of the variables studied. In many cases these responses will be in coded narrative form. In quantitative studies

you use tests, scales, surveys, questionnaires, completion of projects, or reports. Some studies combine both kinds of research. If you wish your readers to see your instruments or measures in their totality, they can be included in an appendix. Your obligation in the method section of the paper is to ensure that the reader understands what measures you used and how you gathered the information. The process of collection needs to be clearly stated and how it was stored also needs to be explained. You may want to establish the validity and reliability of your measures if they are expected or required. This is particularly necessary if you have developed your own instruments and if you are doing a quantitative study.

Data Analysis

Your task in this part of the method section is to define the methods, measures, and processes used to analyze the data you have collected. If you are doing a quantitative study or are involved in an experimental, empirical, and statistical study, you will be using scales, tests, surveys, and questionnaires for gathering your data. You need to define the statistical analyses used whether they be descriptive statistical analyses, correlational statistical analyses, inferential statistical analyses, or a combination of these statistical measures. If you are using descriptive statistical analyses you may be using mean, median, mode, average mean gain, range, and standard deviation. If you are using inferential statistical analyses the most commonly used are the *t* test and chi square to measure for significance although there are many other inferential analyses. You may use the Pearson *r* or other measures for correlational analyses. There are many statistical measures available for analysis of data. You need to select those most appropriate for your study.

If you are doing a qualitative study you are focusing on the nature or essence of the population in terms of the variables tested. You need to identify how you coded materials gathered data, identified recurrent patterns, commonalities, and differences, including how you

analyzed and examined those generalizations. This is usually done in a detailed narrative form in qualitative studies. You will also need to relate how the study evolved during its duration. You will need to determine if any grounded or substantive theory emerged from the study. You, as the researcher, are the primary instrument in data collection. These are the expectations your reader can have in this part of the method section in qualitative studies

Assessment and Evaluation

You have finished your category on data analysis. In terms of assessment and evaluation you discuss the formative and summative processes in terms of their generalizability, replication, and their application to other similar populations or even different populations. You may also need to address how the final report will be prepared and to whom it is to be distributed. You have the obligation in this part of the method section to bring the process together in a final statement about the study and what it means. You need here to describe both the formative and summative processes in terms of how the study progressed and what the issues and problems were that arose during the process. This is particularly important for qualitative studies and needs to be included in the narrative. The assessment and evaluation component is not a statement of findings, but is your final statement about the study itself. It is the summary of the process both formative and summative of how you arrived at your findings.

Writing Tips

The writing style of the method section is the same as it is in the other sections of your study. You seek for clarity and a cogent presentation of the narrative. You need to include enough detail so that the reader clearly understands the content of each of the categories. You should also remember that everything in the method section is written in the past tense or in the present perfect tense. This section is more technical in some respects than the introduction and review of literature and you should pay close attention to the information you present and how

you present it. This section usually contains terminology that is specific to the study and statistical terms that are not always reader friendly. You should, therefore, write in simple sentences with an economy of expression, carefully wrought syntax, and with a studied clarity. Verbosity, as you know, is the last refuge of mediocrity. You are writing for your peers, but even so, you may need to explain some terms that are specific to your study. You will also be using more professional terminology in this section than in the previous sections. Make sure the technical terminology is in context and is made as clear as possible to the reader. Some of your categories in this method section may be relatively brief. Make sure, however, that all the information needed is presented in a sequential and logical manner. Your obligation is to ensure the writing fully expresses the nature of the study and the logical development of the process you used in conducting the study. Write without personal commentary. You simply report how the study was done. This is the essence of the writing process for this section of your paper.

For a quick review of the elements necessary to the this section of your paper refer to the checklist for the method section in Appendix A on page 76. Use this checklist to ensure that you have included all the expected components of the method section.

Preparing the Results

In the results section, if it is required, you report your findings based on the data you have collected. In the method section, you have noted how the data was collected, what instruments were used and what statistical measures or qualitative analyses were used. In the results section, you report on the outcomes of those analyses. You do nothing more. Implications, conclusions, and recommendations are reserved for the discussion section of the study. There are two kinds of research studies which are discussed in this work. One is a quantitative study and the second is a qualitative study. Some researchers may use both in a single study. Each of these kinds of research study requires a different sequence and content for the results section and for the researcher/writer. The sequences for each kind of study are presented below.

Quantitative Results

In quantitative studies you are presenting a study based on a statistical analysis of the data collected. In your method section you identified the population, the variables to be tested, the instruments you used, and the statistical measures used to analyze the data. You will need to briefly review this information for the results section of your study. Once this is done, you present the results. If your study is experimental you are reporting how the intervention or treatment impacted the experimental group compared to the control group. This can be done through reporting descriptive statistical results, correlational statistical results, or inferential statistical results. You may also need to use more than one of these statistical approaches in your analysis of results Descriptive measures are used to determine mean, median, mode, range, average mean gain, and standard deviation. Inferential statistical measures are used to determine significance. The most commonly measures used in inferential analyses are the t test and chi square. If you are using a pre test or post test as your instruments to obtain results, questions of

reliability and validity may arise. Be sure, whenever necessary, to respond to those questions with the data the readers expect. Correlational statistical analyses are used to show relationships among or between variables. Correlational studies are either predictive or relational and are used to establish a correlational coefficient between or among the variables used. One common correlation measure used for analysis is the Pearson product-moment coefficient or Pearson r. You need to choose the statistical measures pertinent to your study. Some formal studies are based on descriptive statistical analysis, but most researchers use other measures while at times also using descriptive statistics as well. Think through what you are studying and then determine the statistical measures appropriate to that study. In organizing the results you need to consider the variables being tested and how best to report results in terms of those variables. You can report which variable results were more significant than others, but with no personal commentary. Descriptive statistical analyses are relatively easy to do, but are not as powerful as correlational statistical analyses or inferential statistical analyses. Many graduate students use descriptive statistical measures particularly if the time frame for the study is narrow. If, however, you are going to report significance or lack of significance in your quantitative study you will need to use inferential statistical analyses. If you are reporting how variables correlated with others you use correlational analyses. In both of these statistical analyses you will need to report the level of confidence or significance of the results. These results can be shown through figures or tables included in the narrative. They may also be placed in an appendix. In this section of your work, only the results should be reported. There must be no personal commentary, interpretation, or conclusions about the results. Here you report only on the outcomes and results of your statistical analyses. These are the final results of what you have done and what happened through your study. This section needs to be a cogently and clearly written part of your paper.

Reporting variables. When you are reporting your findings about individual variables you should identify the variable and then provide the results of your analyses of that variable. This is important to do this because the reader needs to know for which variable or variables you are providing results. Each variable represents, in most cases, data that can be disaggregated according to the demographics of the population involved in the study. Use as much detail as is necessary. The reader will need to know precisely what you have found. The reader needs to know this both in terms of the totality of the data and in terms of data which has been disaggregated for identified groups within the population. You must provide the results accurately and clearly. Sometimes you may want to include figures, graphs, or tables to visually present your results. These can be written as part of the narrative or they can be placed in the appendix. If they are in the appendix, let the reader know by a notation in the narrative.

Surveys, questionnaires, interviews. If you have used a survey, questionnaire, or interviews as the measure for data collection, you usually will have a large number of variables you could use for study. These variables emerge from the demographic data in the survey, questionnaire or interviews. You select the variables that are most specific to the purpose of the study. The variables selected should reflect those that are the most important and best illustrate the questions or issues you are investigating. Demographic variables may include age, length of service, assignment, education, gender, and ethnicity. These demographic variables can be used to disaggregate the data in terms of results. When reporting the results from the survey, questionnaire, or interview, write the statement exactly as it appears on the instrument. This statement is then followed by a report of the results in terms of each selected variable using the statistical measures you used to analyze responses to that variable. As the researcher, you may select some of the statements for detailed inclusion in the results. If you do so, you must

provide a rationale for your choice of statements and provide a summary of the data from the remaining statements immediately following the analysis of the selected variables. If, in your survey or questionnaire you may have included a space for comments. You need to include pertinent comments in your study. These selected comments are listed immediately following your analysis of the data from the survey or questionnaire and the summary of the statements or questions not analyzed. Sometimes you may wish to have a space for comments after each statement on a survey or a question on a questionnaire. If this is so, the comments can be linked directly to the statement or question. Following your presentation of the results from selected variables, statements, and the summary of the results from the variables, you must prepare a summative statement about the results. This summative statement is designed to bring together the results in a brief way to review the totality of the results and to ensure that the reader has one more opportunity to review the study in terms of the all the results determined through your analyses. This summative statement does not have to be lengthy. If you have determined significance, be sure to report it. Include evidence of variance in terms of demographics and specific variables This summative statement should be brief, but with enough detail to ensure the reader clearly understands your results You will interpret the meaning of the results in the discussion section of the paper. If you have any questions about how to develop a survey or questionnaire see Appendix F.

Qualitative Results

First, the researcher needs to review the process of data collection as noted in the method section and to explain to the reader how the data was collected and analyzed. In qualitative studies you will be dealing with a large amount of data, much of it narrative data, collected through the various observations, interviews and other measures you used. In qualitative studies, you analyze these data. As researcher, you are responsible for the rich thick narrative that tells

about both the formative and summative development of the study. Your narrative and findings should be comprehensive, expansive, and richly descriptive. You may need to code or categorize your data as the project develops. These codes or categories can develop and change as the study develops. Be sure to keep a detailed record of what has happened in the study on a daily or regular basis. The information you have gathered in the codes and categories can ensure that the detailed record of your study can be verified. As part of the narrative you may want to use figures or tables. You can do this as part of the narrative. You may also place figures and tables in an appendix. Be sure to follow APA guidelines for figures and tables. Through the process of analysis you have developed generalizations about the data. Your analyses and results have been gained throughout the qualitative process, but the results will be a synthesis of the generalizations in a descriptive narrative or an emerging theory grounded in the data you have collected. The mode of analysis in qualitative studies is inductive and is done by the researcher. From these generalizations, from the descriptive narrative, and from the emerging theory you have results that can provide meaning and substance for your colleagues. The descriptive narrative must be as complete as possible. Some deem it a richly descriptive narrative (Merriam, 1998). You are narrating the totality of the process involved in your study as well as the emerging information and grounded theory in this narrative. You inform the reader with clarity and a continuity the meaning of the study in terms of results which may include grounded theory. This is as far as you go in this section of your study. You write clearly, but include all the narrative and all the details necessary. Your narrative establishes the basis for conclusions and recommendations that are made in the discussion section of the paper. For further study you may wish to use descriptive, inferential or correlational statistical analyses with your data. Generalizability and application to similar populations are reserved for the discussion section of the paper.

Writing Tips

Again, when you are writing the results, you are dealing with technical terms as well as mathematical and statistical terms in quantitative studies. In qualitative studies you are dealing with narrative results and emerging theory. You may also be dealing with statistical data and analyses in qualitative studies if they need to be used. You need, however, to make these narrative results clear to the reader. In quantitative studies you must make sure that the reader does not get confused by the narrative, the terms, and the organization of the results. Results of the analysis of each variable should be discussed in simple terms within the narrative as well as in any figures or tables. The numbers need to be presented succinctly and clearly. Avoid simply presenting numbers and statistical data. If you are comparing results in variables make sure you clearly state what you are doing and why you are doing it. You may need to present the numbers, the data, and the comparisons in a figure or table so they can be seen and more easily understood by the reader. You may include the figures or tables in the text or place them in an appendix. Make sure your explanation of the results is organized and sequenced in a simple and logical order that makes sense to the reader. You may have to work on this explanation to make it readable and cogent for the reader. An introductory paragraph to the results section to inform the reader how you have organized the results including which statements or questions will be specifically analyzed and how you will organize the results section can be very helpful in orienting the reader to a clearer construct of the results section. Results must be understood to be used by your readers. Write your quantitative results in past or present perfect tense.

In qualitative studies you prepare a narrative of the results. The narrative is written in past tense or present perfect tense. An introductory paragraph on how you organized this section could be included, but may not be necessary. You must make sure that the reader understands how you developed your generalizations and how the theory emerged from the

narrative. Great care must be taken in qualitative studies to ensure that the narrative has substance and meaning. You must make sure the findings and results are grounded in the data and that the inferences and emerging theory are logical and provide an evidentiary base. If you use figures or tables as part of your results, be sure to follow APA guidelines. In writing this narrative, the researcher must be sure that no bias, interpretation, or personal perspectives are apparent. These are included only in the discussion section of your paper. In writing the results in both quantitative and qualitative studies, be sure that you have written with clarity, with cohesiveness, and in a cogent and careful manner. Use the past or present perfect tense in writing the results section of your study.

For a quick review of the elements necessary for inclusion in the results section refer to the checklist for the results section in Appendix A on page 77. The use of this checklist can help to ensure that you have included all components required in the results section for your study.

Preparing the Discussion

This is the final narrative section of your paper. It is titled discussion with that word centered one double space below the page header. In this *Handbook* the presentation of the discussion section of the paper is in two parts depending on whether you are writing a review of literature paper or a research study. For both types of papers there is a summary of the content of the discussion of the literature reviewed and presented in the content of the review of literature. For a research study, there is a summary of both the review of literature, the method, and the results in the content of the discussion. Much of the content in both kinds of papers is similar, but there are some differences. In both types you follow the summary of the literature reviewed with your interpretation. Finally for both kinds of papers you would draw conclusions and develop recommendations based on the content of the review of literature and your interpretation. In research studies you compare and contrast the findings of your study with corollary studies in the review of literature and then write your conclusions and recommendations. In either type of paper, you could write this section in narrative form without separating it into its component parts, though you may want to organize it into the component parts of summary, interpretation, conclusions, and recommendations. It is important that you remember that this is your final narrative section of the paper and that it needs, like all the other sections, to be written clearly, carefully, and cogently.

Review of Literature Paper

In a review of literature paper you do these four things. First, you summarize the literature you have reviewed. Second, you interpret the literature reviewed. Third, you draw conclusions based on your interpretation and the content of the review, and fourth you make recommendations. This is the sequence of the discussion section in the review of literature papers. Follow this sequence. Do not change the order. Do not bring in any new resources,

citations, or additional references in this section of the paper. Those were all done in the review of literature.

Summary. Your first task in the discussion is to summarize the literature you reviewed. In a paragraph or a few paragraphs correlated with your categories summarize what you learned from the review of literature. This summary is a recap to help the reader in understanding the interpretation which comes next and to succinctly bring out the salient points of the review of literature. You will need to cite sources so the reader can better understand source of the information. The sources you cite should be your most important sources and should relate to the salient points you want to make in the interpretation. You may use the same or similar ones in the interpretation. Do not add anything more to the summary. Do not cite new sources in the summary. The summary is written in the past tense or present perfect tense without comment. It is a succinct review of the most important things you found in the review of literature that pertain directly to the purpose of your paper.

Interpretation. This is the part of the discussion where you give your own interpretation and opinion about the literature you reviewed. Here you emphasize what you agree with and with what you disagree. You interpret, you compare and contrast, and you bridge the gaps. You give opinions and insights about the literature you reviewed. In the interpretation you provide the reader with your own perspective about the literature reviewed. This part of the discussion must be carefully constructed because your interpretations, insights, linkages, and opinions provide the basis for your conclusions and recommendations. The evidence you have brought forward in your review of literature and that you have summarized in this discussion provide, along with your interpretation, the evidentiary and logical rationale for your conclusions and for your recommendations. Do not go into great detail. Keep the commentary focused on the literature and your interpretation of that literature. Do not be redundant. Your interpretation

must be soundly based on what you have reported in the review of literature. You may write the interpretation in present tense. Think very carefully about what you want to say and how you have thought through the literature so you can write a logical and substantive interpretation that will be clear to the reader and provide the basis for your conclusions and recommendations. You need to ensure that the literature reviewed provided an evidentiary base for your conclusions and recommendations.

Conclusions. The conclusions you have drawn from your review of literature and your interpretation do not need to be lengthy. A sentence like "based on the review of literature and my interpretation of the literature, I have concluded that. . . ." Then you list your conclusions with little elaboration. The conclusions should be written in simple sentences and as briefly and efficiently as possible. You need only enough words to make your conclusion clear. You do not need to go into long or even brief explanations of the conclusions. That was done in the interpretation part of the discussion. Your conclusions should stand alone as the summative statements about what you have concluded and what the reader should also conclude. The rationale and evidentiary base for your conclusions was made apparent in the interpretation.

Recommendations. Recommendations are statements about what should be done, what should be implemented, or what changes should be made based on your review of literature, interpretations, and conclusions. Recommendations, like the conclusions, should not be lengthy or complex. They should draw their evidentiary base from the literature, the interpretation and the conclusions. Recommendations should be written in the same manner as suggested above in the conclusions statement. Almost all papers need recommendations, only a few do not. For review of literature papers this is the final narrative statement of your paper. Do not go into an elaboration, or an explanation. Do not add any new material. State what you recommend as the last narrative statement of your paper. Succinctly stated and carefully written, recommendations

can bring a strong closing to your paper.

For a quick review of the elements necessary for the discussion section of review of literature papers refer to the checklist in Appendix A on page 78. The use of this checklist will help ensure that you have included the required elements of the discussion section in your paper.

Research Studies

In the discussion section of a research study whether quantitative or qualitative, you follow the same structure and organization noted for review of literature papers. You summarize, next you interpret, then you draw conclusions, and finally you make recommendations. The organization is the same, but the content varies somewhat. Your obligation in the discussion of research studies is to summarize your findings and how they relate to the literature. You must ensure that your review of literature provided an evidentiary base for your conclusions and that the review included research studies related to your topic. If you have done this, you are ready to interpret the literature. In your interpretation You discuss the literature, your method, and your results. As you reviewed research studies related to your area of study you can interpret your method and results in terms of those studies. You then draw conclusions and make recommendations on the basis of the literature, the method, and of the results of your study. This chapter or section of your paper is of great importance because you are presenting a professional discussion of what you learned, how you interpreted it, and what you concluded and recommended. This is the final and summative statement of what you have done. You have completed a research study that has importance in your field and you need to disseminate it clearly and with emphasis on what it means to you and to your colleagues in the profession.

Summary. In this summary component of results you do two things. You summarize the review of literature and your findings. In the review of literature you focused on the works of

researchers and important sources in your particular area of study. You have prepared the review of literature in terms of the purpose of your study and here you summarize the salient points of that review in terms of the focus and purpose of the study. You then summarize your method and results in terms of the studies you have reviewed. Your summary of results is a summative statement and should include your most pertinent findings. Once you have stated your results you need to summarize the literature related to your study. Make sure you have included a summary of studies related to your purpose including their methods and findings. You should focus only the major sources and research studies closely related to your study. You will need to include citations so readers know your major sources. Do not bring in any new sources here, you are simply summarizing your findings and the review of literature. Remember not to interpret nor elaborate on any findings nor any literature in this section of results. Simply tell what you found and identify and summarize the literature closely related to your study. This summary of literature reviewed should be used in conjunction with the results from your study. The summary should be written in the past tense or present perfect tense

Interpretation. Here you present your own views on what you have done and what your results mean both in terms of your study and in terms of related literature and other studies in the field. Note how your study related to or correlated with other studies in the field. Show where and how you method and findings agreed were similar to or different from other studies. You compare and contrast, you interpret similarities and differences, and you bridge the gaps. You may include in your narrative figures, tables, and graphs as needed to visually show your results. These would be figures, tables, and graphs already introduced in the results section. From your study do not include new tables, figures or graphs. You can also include figures, tables, and graphs from prior studies specific to your study. They can be introduced in this section of the study. These figures, tables, and graphs could also be placed in an appendix. Discuss any

theories or ideas that you have confirmed or where your findings were consistent or not consistent with other studies. You compare and contrast your findings with other research in the field and interpret similarities and differences. You must identify significance or lack of significance in terms of the variables tested in quantitative studies if you are using inferential statistical measures. If you are using correlational statistical measures you need to show how identified variables correlate or do not correlate. You must point out in qualitative studies your generalizations and any grounded theory that emerged. You need to emphasize how your results fit into other studies and literature in the field. The interpretation component of the discussion is extremely important. You write it with care and concern because the successful dissemination of your findings will be based largely on this section of the paper. The generalizability of your results for other similar populations will be based on this interpretation of your study.

As you write the interpretation, readers need to clearly understand what you have found and how your findings relate to the area of study. You emphasize in your closing paragraphs what you feel are the most important findings and the points that highlight what you consider to be important for your colleagues in the field. Be as direct as you need and emphasize the importance of those findings. The final paragraphs of your interpretation should contain the summative statement of your findings, their importance, and how they relate to the area of study. It is from these culminating evidentiary statements in the interpretation that you draw your conclusions and your recommendations.

Conclusions. Your conclusions are drawn directly from the review of literature and the interpretation of the literature, the method, and the results. They should be linked to the summative statements in your interpretation. Conclusions should be written clearly and with the use of only the words needed to state what you have concluded. Conclusions are not lengthy, nor are they convoluted. They are concise and straight forward statements. Conclusions should

reflect what you found and carry the conclusive message of your paper. A sentence beginning "based on the review of literature and the findings of this study I have concluded that. . . ." This is all that is needed. Do not elaborate or explain. That was done in the interpretation. Both quantitative and qualitative studies follow this pattern. In qualitative studies you should note any grounded theory emerging from your study. Nothing further needs to be written.

Recommendations. Your recommendations are based on your results, your review of literature, your interpretation, and your conclusions. A recommendation is your statement about what you feel needs yet to be done, on generalizability to specific groups, or on further research that should be done in the area of the study. You are making your last narrative statement of the study and your conclusions and recommendations are the final comments you make. Recommendations should be cast in clear, concise, and confident language and attest to a job well done. You do not need to explain the recommendations or elaborate on them. They are your final succinct statements of a study done with care and attention to the process and to the outcomes. Recommendations are what you project for future studies or for implementation of results.

For a quick review of the expected elements of the discussion section of a research study refer to the checklist in Appendix A on page 79. The use of this checklist will help ensure that you have included all the required components of this section of your research study.

Writing Tips

These writing tips apply to both review of literature papers and to research studies except where noted. The discussion section of the paper can be written as a narrative without categories and subcategories or you can organize it with categories. If your paper is relatively brief, do not organize this section into categories. If you use categories you can name them summary, interpretation, conclusions, and recommendations. Subcategories in a research study

could be the names of the categories of your method section such as population, variables, analyses and so forth. If you choose to have categories and subcategories you will need to follow APA guidelines. In almost every case you will not use subcategories.

In this final section of the paper or study you will continue to use citations to keep the reader informed about the sources to which you are referring. Citations are necessary only in the summary and interpretation components of the discussion. They should not be used for conclusions or recommendations Do not introduce any new sources in the discsussion. Be sure to use the APA style and format for all citations. All of your citations should refer to sources within the review of literature. In this section you point out what was most important in the literature as it relates to your interpretation. In a research study you also need to identify your findings and interpret them as they relate to the literature you reviewed. In both quantitative and qualitative studies you express your own opinion in the interpretation components of this discussion section. Express your personal opinions along with your conclusions and recommendations. This chapter or section is the only place in the paper or study where you present personal opinions and interpretations. This is where you can be emphatic and confident. This is where you make the final determination about the importance and worth of your paper or study. Make sure that the final paragraphs in the interpretation clearly state what you consider to be most important to the reader. This becomes the link to your conclusions and your recommendations.

While some of the writing in this section is in the past tense or present perfect tense, in particular the summary, you can present your interpretations, opinions, conclusions, and recommendations in the present tense. Your recommendations can, in some instances, be in the future tense. In the discussion you present your summary and findings. You also tell the reader how you interpreted the literature and the findings. In terms of your findings you both interpret

them and suggest meanings. Be sure that the meaning of the study is consistent with the results. In the interpretation you also need to compare and contrast your findings with related studies you reviewed. The review of literature should provide an integral part of the evidentiary base for your study. This is also where you present your opinions. In the discussion is you compare and contrast, bridge the gaps, judge and interpret. Here is where you conclude and where you recommend. Indeed, this is what the discussion is all about.

In the interpretation component of the discussion you can use the personal pronoun I or if there is more than one author the personal pronoun we. It is wise, however, to minimize the use of I or we. Let what has been written speak for itself. Do not, however, refer to yourself as the author. You can also write in the present tense except in the summary. When you make recommendations you may, if appropriate, use the future tense. You have the opportunity, in this section, to reflect you personal perspectives and opinions. You will strongly support your professional findings and positions in terms of the interpretation, conclusions, and recommendations as long as they are supported by evidence from the review of literature and from the results. This is where you react to the issues, problems, and questions inherent within the paper. You do this based on the review of literature and the findings if you did a research paper. You do not bring in any new resources. What you have done needs to rest on its own integrity. You present your paper from your own professional perspective.

When you have completed this section of the paper you have finished a well organized and properly sequenced professional paper. Be sure to edit it and refine the rough drafts. One good way to do this is to read it aloud. You can quickly hear problems of organization, continuity, and syntax, and make the necessary corrections. Another good way to edit the paper is to have a peer or someone else critique it. Be sure to find someone who will be objective and provide positive suggestions and ideas for you in terms of editing your paper. Once the final

editing is done, you will have completed the professional preparation of your paper. It will be ready for a professional reader to review it and ready for publication.

In writing your paper, do not procrastinate. Start as soon as you have defined the topic. Define the topic as quickly as possible. You know that you have a deadline to meet, so follow a schedule. Sometimes the schedule may be set by the instructor. Sometimes you need to develop a personal timeline for completion of the paper or study. Above all, do not wait until late in the class time frame or the report schedule to start your paper. In some instances the instructor or supervisor may be willing to review your paper or consult with you if you have any problems. Take advantage of those reviews and consultations. If your instructor or supervisor will review the paper, turn in a rough draft or what you have completed at the time designated by the instructor or supervisor. The review by the instructor or supervisor as well as consultations with others can help you produce a much better paper, perhaps one that will be published in some context.

Just a word about plagiarism. Remember that you can use direct quotes, paraphrase, and summarize a writer's work. You must, however, always cite the source. Using an author's words directly without citation constitutes plagiarism and will result in a seriously marred paper or a failing grade. Your reader will check for plagiarism. Start gathering resources in an organized manner. Note all the bibliographical information for any source reviewed and cited in your paper. Annotate pertinent resources. Also write down appropriate quotes and key them to page numbers. Cite them in your paper. Once you have identified the categories, put your sources along with quotes and bibliographical information in categories or on colored cards so they are keyed to your categories. Develop a personal system for organizing and categorizing information. In writing your paper, set a time line and keep to it. Build into the time line checkpoints and benchmarks for completing certain sections and for editing purposes. Formal papers take

consistent and careful effort and time.   Be sure that you put in as much time as you will need. Keep this *Handbook* close by for reference and as a resource for writing your paper. Best wishes to you in your writing process and congratulations on finishing this last narrative section of your paper.

Preparing the References

The final section of your paper is the reference section. This section is titled references. It is not a part of the narrative, but it is an integral and essential section of your paper and is numbered as part of the paper with a page header. In this section you include only the references you have cited in the paper. Do not include any other references. This is not a bibliography. It is a list of sources you have referred to in your paper. Be sure that every entry and every line in the reference section is double spaced Your reader will check the citations and references carefully and match them with each other. Your reader will also check to ensure that you have followed the format of the APA. It is, therefore, essential that you follow the APA format. You will find clear and specific formats for all kinds of references in the *Publication Manual of the American Psychological Association.* A list of the most common references is also provided for you in the Appendix E beginning on page 89 of this handbook. It should be noted here that personal communications are not included in the reference section. See page 55 for a discussion of how to format them. Personal communications are included only in the narrative sections of the paper, not in the reference section. You must ensure that all references are alphabetized by author. If no author is listed for the source, the title of the source is used. If there is no title a concise descriptor of the source is used. Again, all references are listed in alphabetic sequence including those without an author named. The reference format is called a hanging reference. This means that the first line of each reference is justified to the left margin. Succeeding lines in the reference are tabbed with the same number of spaces you used for the paper. If you are referencing an internet source, include the pathway and be sure the pathway is not underlined and that it is always written in black with an APA approved typeface. Do not put a period after the pathway unless it is a part of it. You must also include the date you downloaded or reviewed the internet source. The references for this work are found on page 67. This is an example of how

your reference section should be organized and formatted.

For a quick review of the elements of the reference section, please refer to the checklist for references found in Appendix A on page 80. The use of this checklist will help ensure that you have completed the required components of the reference section.

Bibliography and Appendixes

It should be noted here that you may include a bibliography and appendixes in your paper. These are not essential elements of the paper, but you may want to include them if you feel they are needed. A bibliography is a list of resources not in the references, but which pertain to the topic or the study. Do not include sources that do not correlate with your topic or to your study. The bibliography is not a part of your narrative paper, nor is it a part of the reference section. If you include a bibliography as additional source material, it is a good idea to do a brief annotation of each resource so the reader can select material of interest that will provide for supplemental personal reading in the field. The annotation is blocked and begins one double space below the entry. It is not indented. The bibliography immediately follows the reference section of your paper. A bibliography has a page header for each page and is sequenced with the paper or the study.

Appendixes, if you have included them, are placed following the reference section of your paper and the bibliography if one is included. When there is more than one appendix, they are usually lettered A, B, C, D and so forth. If the paper has only one appendix, it is simply referred to as the appendix. Each appendix must have a title. Appendixes may include tables, figures, statistical information, illustrations or narrative, and any additional supplemental material you feel is important for reader information. In the body of the paper, usually in the method, the results, or in the discussion sections, you can refer to the appendix pertinent to the information or to the interpretation presented. Be sure to follow APA style and format for all appendixes.

For a quick review of the elements of the bibliography see the checklist for bibliography in Appendix A page 83. For a review of the elements of appendixes refer to the checklist for appendixes in Appendix A page 82. The use of these checklists will help ensure that you have completed the required components of the bibliography and the appendix in the correct format.

Common Problems in Writing Formal Papers

Over the years we have read thousands of formal papers. We are, here, focusing on some of the more common errors, problems, and issues we have found in student writing. The *Publication Manual of the American Psychological Association* provides an excellent source for helping you in the writing process. This *Handbook* is consistent with that manual. There are other fine manuals and resources available to you as well, some of which we have already cited. What we have done here, however, is to provide a compendium of common problems, issues, and errors in graduate and formal papers we have read over the past years. They are listed in alphabetic order. We consistently find these errors in papers. Be cognizant of them as you write your own paper.

Abstract. The abstract is noted as page two of your paper. It consists of from 120 to 150 words and includes the purpose of the paper or study and salient points you have found. Major findings, if you have written a research study, are included. Conclusions and recommendations should also be included. The abstract is not indented; it is blocked.

Agreement. Referents should agree in gender and number. This statement encapsulates the nature of these kinds of errors. Verbs and pronouns should agree in gender and number with the subject. In this era of politically correct writing, we have frequently read papers where the author has used a single subject such as student and has then used they, their, or them rather than having noun pronoun agreement. This is not acceptable in formal papers. You can use he/she if you wish, but avoid this as much as possible. In most instances you can, through careful writing, avoid the heeshees and remain consistent in terms of subject pronoun agreement. There should also be agreement in gender and number with subject and verb. Review your paper carefully to correct any such errors.

Among and between. You should note that when you are comparing and contrasting or

making a statement discussing difference between pairs and groups you use *among* when referring to more than two or more than groups of two. You use *between* when referring only to groups of two or to pairs of groups.

Anthropomorphisms. An anthropomorphism occurs when ascribing human characteristics to animals or inanimate objects. Remember that research cannot say, infer, demonstrate, show, or indicate. Only researchers, writers, or authors can write, infer, demonstrate, show, or indicate. This is a very common error by writers of formal papers including some which occur in published papers and books. Avoid anthropomorphisms. They indicate sloppiness of style and careless construction.

Author reference. Use the personal pronoun I with great care throughout the paper. Do not use the third person or refer to yourself as the author of the paper. Whenever you need to refer to yourself use the personal pronoun I. If the paper has two or more authors use we. Minimize the use of I throughout the paper. Use it when you note why I chose the paper in the introduction and when you interpret, conclude, and recommend in the discussion section. It is seldom, if ever, used in other sections of the paper.

Categories. These categories represent the major parts of any narrative section of your paper. They are most frequently used in the review of literature, but can be used in other sections of your paper or study as needed. Other than in the review of literature, if your paper is relatively brief, you may not need to use them. The name of the category is in italics and is on a separate line in the narrative. Keep the names of the categories as brief as possible. You must have at least two categories in any section of the paper to justify their use.

Citations. Citations are simple to do, but if in doubt refer to the APA *Manual.* The usual citation is the author's last name followed by a comma and the year of publication. If no date of publication is given use the initials n.d. in lower case. This information is in parentheses. You

may use the author's name as part of a sentence. If you do, follow it with the year of publication in parentheses. When a work has no author use the first two words of the title. If there is no author or title use a brief descriptor of the content not to exceed two words. These are the first two words of your reference. If you are using a direct quote, you must use the author's name, the year, and the page number of the quotation. Direct quotes of less than forty words require quotation marks. Direct quotes of forty or more words are blocked without the use of quotation marks. If the quote is from a short internet article use the abbreviation para. followed by the paragraph number. You may also use the paragraph symbol. Check the most recent edition of the APA *Manual* for additional information on electronic citations and references.

Colloquialisms. Avoid the use of colloquial language. In a formal paper, this is unacceptable except in rare circumstances or unless the colloquialism occurs in a direct quote. A colloquialism is informal or idiomatic speech or writing and should not be used in formal papers. The most common colloquialism we have seen in papers is "a lot" meaning many or frequent. Writers forget that a lot is a small area of ground on which structures can be built. Avoid also the use of idioms and slang expressions.

Ellipses. An ellipsis is used when you leave a word or words out of a direct quote for clarity of meaning. An ellipsis is shown by three dots to signify that a word or words have been omitted from the quote. You make an ellipsis by doing a dot with a space between dots three times to show words omitted. Use four dots with a space between each dot when the omitted words occur in two or more sentences. Generally do not begin or end a quote with ellipses.

Hyphens. Do not end a line or begin a line of the narrative with a hyphen. Use hyphens as defined by the APA. Self, when it is linked to a characteristic is always hyphenated. Non does not need a hyphen. It can stand alone or be linked to its characteristic such as *nondirective.*

If as conditional. When writing in the past tense always use were when following the

noun or pronoun with a past tense form of to be. If, in this sense, is a conditional and requires the use of were.

Justification. The paper is justified only on the left margin. Do not justify on the right margin of the paper. All lines of citations of forty or more words are justified one tab space from the left margin. The right margin in citations is not justified. Only the page header and the numbers of the pages in the table of contents are justified on the right margin. Quotation marks are not used to open or close a block quote. If a quotation is included in a blocked quote use only one quotation mark ('') at the beginning and end of the quote.

Language. Use specific and precise language. Eliminate redundancies. Do not use slang expressions or colloquialisms. Check your choice of words and make sure that you are saying what you want to say with an economy of expression. Say only what needs to be said. Avoid jargon or the continual use of technical language. While some technical or professional terminology may be necessary, the continual use of such language can be distracting and irritating to the reader. Presentation of ideas must be orderly and sequential. Use punctuation to provide clarity and continuity. Use transitional words and pronouns to provide for additional clarity and continuity. Use simple sentences most of the time. Use compound or complex sentences only when necessary.

Numbers. Numbers zero through nine must be written out. Numbers ten and over can be written in their Arabic form. Numbers are always written at the beginning of a sentences such as: Seventy-four percent.

Quotations. There is an expectation that you use direct quotes in your paper. If the quote is less than 40 words it is included in the narrative with quotation marks at the beginning of the quote and at the end of the quote. All quotations must have a citation with a page or paragraph number. For quotations of 40 or more words, each line of the quotation is blocked one tab space

from the left margin. If there is a quotation within the quotation us a single quotation mark ('') at the beginning and end of the quotation.

Personal communications. These refer to people consulted in the preparation of your paper. Personal communications can also be memos, e-mails, and other electronic resources You may quote or paraphrase the information you have gained from them in the narrative sections of your paper. Most frequently these occur in the review of literature. If the personal communication is used for a direct quote follow the format for quotations. Use initials and surname in the citation. Personal communications are cited as follows: J. Doe, (personal communication, June 21, 2005) or (J. W. Doe, personal communication, June 21, 2005) They are cited in the text only and are not included in the reference section.

Plagiarism. Plagiarism means to copy someone's work and claiming it as your own. You must provide a citation for every statement in your paper except the selection of the topic, why you chose the topic, in the interpretion component of the discussion, and in the conclusions, and recommendations. For every other part of the paper you must give credit to the source. Your reader will check for plagiarism. If you have plagiarized content in any part of your paper it will result in a failing grade or a rejection of your paper.

Redundancy. While redundancy may sometimes be used in the discussion section to be emphatic, it should be avoided throughout your paper. Your paper is stronger without it. Do not be emphatic through redundancy. If you wish to emphasize a point in the discussion section, let the reader know that you feel it is important. It may sometimes be necessary to restate an idea, thought, or interpretation for clarity and emphasis, but do it in language different than the original so that it becomes a logical followup to what you have already written.

Referents. Be very careful about referents. Be sure the reader clearly understands what you are referring to when you use a pronoun to refer to the subject. Referent problems occur

most often when you are citing an author and continue discussing the work. Include a restatement of the author's name or the subject of the discussion no later than three to six sentences from the first referent. Referents should agree in gender and number. Do not use we or our to refer to groups of people in your profession. Always use the name of the group of people to whom you are referring.

Spacing. Just a simple reminder. Everything in your paper is double spaced. The use of any other spacing constitutes a format error. The reference section and direct quotes of more than 40 words are double spaced along with every other section of your paper. Text begins one double space below the page header. Improper spacing, as has been noted, is a format error.

Subcategories. The use of subcategories may be necessary, particularly in the review of literature, when you have a category that needs to have more than one area of focus. For example, if you are doing a paper in which one of your categories is instructional strategies, you may have subcategories on each of the specific strategies about which you have reviewed literature. A subcategory is indented one tab space from the left margin. It is written in italics and is followed by a period. The text begins immediately following the notation of the subcategory.

Superscript and subscript. Do not use superscript or subscript except in mathematical or scientific formulae or as approved by the APA. Do not use superscript in the reference section when referring to the edition of a book.

Syntax. Sentence structure is important. Write clearly, sequentially, and logically. Use simple sentences for the most part. Say only what needs to be said. Compound and complex sentences should be used only when needed and to clarify the information presented. Comma splices (sometimes called comma faults), run on sentences, and fragments are major syntax errors and could seriously affect the quality of your paper and your grade. Major syntax errors would

certainly be noted by an editor or publisher. Fragments occur most frequently when you begin a sentence with an adverb. Be sure to review your paper for syntax errors.

Tense. This is one of the most common errors we have seen in papers. In formal papers you use the past tense or the present perfect tense consistently in the abstract, introduction, and review of literature. You also use the past or present perfect tense in the method and results sections of a research study. The present perfect tense refers to an action that did not occur at a specific defined time or occurred in the past and is continuing. Remember that when the reader reviews your paper you have already completed the paper. All literature or research you cite in your paper has been completed. The only exception for the use of the past or present perfect tense is within direct quotes when the writer you are quoting uses a tense other than the past tense or present perfect tense. In the discussion section of your paper you use the past tense or present perfect tense in the summary or when referring to the literature reviewed. You may use the present tense, the future tense, or other tenses when you are interpreting, comparing and contrasting, expressing your professional opinions, drawing conclusions or making recommendations.

That and who. Use who or whom to refer to humans. Use that or which to refer to animals. This is a frequent error and needs to be avoided.

Typeface. Use only typefaces approved by the APA. You must use 12 point size only. APA recommends Times Roman, Courier, or similar. No superscript or subscript may be used except in specified scientific or mathematics symbols or formulae. Do not use superscript in the reference section. Eliminate any color other than black in the reference section including internet pathways.

Voice. Use the active voice rather than the passive voice in your writing in most instances. The active voice is a direct communicator of ideas and meaning and the active voice

fits well into the context of formal papers. The passive voice is used only when you want to focus on the object of the action or the recipient of the action. Proper use of voice makes for clearer communication of the content of your paper

Formal Writing Conventions

Formal writing is a style used by those who are preparing papers, reviews of literature, research studies, and formal documents for a specific audience. As noted in the preface, formal writing is a pristine exercise in clarity, continuity, and cogent thinking. Conventions of formal writing ensure that this occurs in papers, documents, and research studies. Formal writing is consistently used when writing a review of literature paper or a research study. Formal writing is used for some reports, for monographs, and for a variety of other formal documents. Formal writing can also be used for preparing narrative journal articles or formal reports to designated groups. Formal writing is a style that can be easily learned. It does, however, have certain conventions which need to be followed and used in the preparation of the document you plan to submit. Listed below are some of the conventions of formal writing.

Organization

Formal writing is organized into sections or chapters according to the length of the paper. Generally in papers under fifty pages one does not use chapters. Use section headings. For longer papers, monographs, or narrative documents chapters may be used as headings with the title of the chapter centered one double space below the number of the chapter which is written in upper case Roman numerals. When writing a review of literature paper, three sections will be used. They are introduction, review of literature, and discussion. The full title of the paper is used in the introduction. The next sections are entitled review of literature and discussion. For research studies there are five sections. They are introduction, review of literature, method, results, and discussion. The full title is used in the introduction. The succeeding sections are entitled as review of literature, method, results, and discussion. For theses or dissertations of more than fifty pages, these five sections can be noted as chapters. In writing formal papers for journals, these sections may not be necessary. For formal reports and documents, follow a

narrative sequence or any structure set by the organization to which the document or formal report is to be submitted. An abstract of from 120-150 words follows the title page and precedes content. A table of contents may be expected, particularly in research studies, monographs, and in some formal reports or documents.

Syntax

Formal writing should be strait forward, strong and cogent. Formal writing should be easily understood by the readers. You are generally writing for audiences familiar with the area of the study or for audiences who want to learn more about the topic or study. Syntax is very important. Most of the time use short simple sentences. Use complex or compound sentences only when necessary. Usually over eighty percent of the sentences should be simple sentences. Use technical language only when needed. The well wrought paper will flow effectively if sentences are clearly understood. Avoid syntactical usage that would result in choppiness and reduce the cogency of the paper. This sometimes happens if only simple sentences are over used. Compound and complex sentences can be used occasionally to make the flow of the paper smoother and more efficient. Do not add extra wording to sentences or try to impress the reader with your erudition. Remember that verbosity is the last refuge of mediocrity. Say only what needs to be said and say it mostly in short, simple, and carefully wrought simple sentences. The appropriate use of syntax can greatly enhance your paper.

Related to syntax is the structure of paragraphs. Paragraphs should not be lengthy. Four to fifteen lines should encompass the length of a paragraph. Paragraphs are organized around a specific topic. Often the topic is stated in the initial sentence, but it can be noted later in the paragraph. The meaning of the paragraph may, however, become apparent only through the whole narrative of the paragraph. The effective use of paragraphs can strengthen the paper and provide for fluent structure, clarity, and sequence for readers.

Word Usage

The selection of the right word is very important in formal writing. Use the precise word in each sentence for clarity of meaning. Keep a dictionary and a thesaurus close by for reference when writing a formal paper. The right words in the right place are strong virtues in formal writing. It is necessary that you avoid colloquialisms, idiomatic expressions, and slang. You are writing a formal paper and the use of those kinds of words or phrases can deter from meaning, bring about an uncomfortable response from the reader, and can reduce the the sequence and flow of the paper. Avoid the use of too many descriptors for nouns. When several descriptors are used, break them out into individual sentences.

It is also very important to avoid value oriented words throughout the paper with the exception of portions of the discussion when interpreting, drawing conclusions, or making recommendations. Even in those portions of the discussion they should be used sparingly, if at all. The use of value oriented words earlier can, and usually do, show your biases and your opinions. These have no place in a formal paper except in the interpretation, conclusions, and recommendations. You are not writing a polemic. You are writing a formal paper that should be as objective as possible until you interpret, analyze, conclude, and recommend. These interpretations, analyses, conclusions, and recommendations are based on your objective review of literature and on the methods and results you have found if you are writing a research paper. As you review your paper, look also for words that are not precise or which can be interpreted in more than one way. Change, if possible, any word that could be interpreted in more than one way. Make changes for precision of language and for the cogency of the paper. The proper use of words is essential in any formal paper.

Tense

The tenses of choice in formal writing are past and present perfect. The past tense is

used consistently throughout the paper for citations and references to the sources you have used. The past tense or present perfect tense are used in every section of the paper with the exception that you may use the present tense or the future tense in the interpretation, conclusion, and recommendation components of the discussion section. The only other exception occurs when a direct quote is used in the paper and contains a tense other than past or present perfect. Present perfect tense is used for an event or issue that started in the past and has been continuing. In the body of the paper the use of past or present perfect is consistent until the discussion section of the paper. In that section the present tense can be used, as noted above, for the interpretation, the conclusions, and the recommendations. When writing the recommendations the future tense may be used. The rationale for using the past tense or present perfect tense is that every source cited or reference has already been written. Even citations from the internet have been posted before you read the paper. A further rationale is that your readers will have read your paper as something that was done in the past and that they are reading from that perspective. This may be one of the conventions that may be the most difficult to accommodate because writers are conditioned to write in the present tense or other tenses. It is important, however that you adhere strictly to this convention when writing formal papers.

Quotations and Paraphrases

Every statement of information in a formal paper with a few exceptions must be based upon the ideas and writings of the authors of your sources. The exceptions in the body of the paper are in the purpose statement and the rationale for selecting topic. Additional exceptions are in the interpretation, conclusions, and recommendations. No opinions, personal perspectives, or added comment can be made in any other section of a formal paper. Every new fact, idea, information, or point of view must come from a source and be cited. Direct quotes from the source may be used. Paraphrases may also be used. They must be cited. Each quotation or

paragraph must have a citation. Direct quotes of less than forty words are shown by quotation marks at the beginning of the quotation and at the end of the quotation. This is followed by the author, the date, and the page number from the source. Quotations of forty or more words are blocked and do not have quotation marks around them Blocked quotes are followed by a citation of the author, year of publication, and page number. You may use paraphrases from a source. These paraphrases must be documented by a citation. Paraphrases are used when you summarizing an author's ideas, narrative, or perspective. Do not add any personal comments or reaction to the paraphrase. You do that in the interpretation component of the discussion section. Your reader will almost always check your sources and will be aware of any personal comments you may have added. It is very important to remember this when writing a formal paper.

References and Bibliography

References and bibliographies are two different elements of a formal paper. References are a compilation of the sources you have cited in the paper. They are listed alphabetically by last name of author. Use only initials for first and middle name. A reference section is required for formal papers in which citations have been made. You need to follow the style manual your university, organization, or corporation recommends. We are using the format provided by the American Psychological Association in their latest publication manual in this *Handbook*. Be sure that you follow the structure of the format for each reference. There are more than a hundred variations and you must select the one that needs to be used for every specific reference. When making citations and preparing for their inclusion in the reference section of the paper, be sure you have all the correct bibliographical information. Many readers will refer to the reference section when citations are made in the body of the work.

Bibliographies are not necessarily a part of a formal paper. They can, however be

included as a separate section following the reference section. A bibliography is an alphabetized list of sources pertinent to the area of study, but not included in the reference section. Do not include any of the sources listed in the reference section of the paper or study. Make sure that the sources listed in the bibliography pertain to the topic of the paper. To ensure that the reader understands this, a brief annotation for each work in the bibliography can be included. We recommend a brief annotation for each listing in the bibliography. Annotations can be brief, but must reflect a relationship to the topic. Bibliographies without annotations can be included, but have little use for the reader. The purpose of the bibliography is to provide the reader with additional sources for further reading and study. We, therefore, strongly recommend an annotated bibliography.

Other Formal Writing Conventions

There are a number of other conventions. Among these are the elimination of anthropomorphisms, the use of the active voice, appropriate use of ellipses, the use of the correct typefaces and font size, the proper use of that and who, among and between, and references to the author. All these and others are discussed in the *Handbook*. Please refer to the section of the *Handbook* which pertains to any questions about these and other formal writing conventions. In the *Handbook* you will not only find information about the writing conventions mentioned above, but useful tips on organization, writing, sequence, and structure. Information you need is also keyed to the page or pages of the *Handbook* where it can be found.

Additional Applications

Formal writing conventions are used in many other contexts. If you are in education and are working on policy or on a committee working on issues of curriculum, instruction, evaluation, policy, or any other issue, formal writing conventions need to be used for any papers to be presented or reports to be prepared. Narrative reports of action research done within the

classroom or the school also need to be written using formal writing conventions. In education, business or other professions, formal writing conventions must be used for white papers, reports, committee summaries, monographs, theses, dissertations, and other formal instruments. The use of formal writing conventions can be applied in any context where there is a need for a clear, concise, and well wrought document. In any of these contexts the use of formal writing conventions can be a responsive and lucid organizational structure available to meet the needs of the writers for their presentations. We encourage the use of these conventions in any professional exercise involving, study, analysis, synthesis, and evaluation. Formal writing conventions can meet the needs of people in any profession and in any circumstance where reporting is needed.

Summary

What we have done in this section of the *Handbook* is to cluster together some of the major conventions of formal writing as well as to briefly refer to others. In some cases this is redundant to what was presented earlier in the *Handbook*. We felt, however, that this reiteration was necessary and positive and would provide a quick overview of formal writing conventions as well as an additional perspective on protocols that must be followed in formal papers. This focus on formal writing conventions provides yet another perspective on developing your formal paper, report, or document. We have provided a brief insight into a number of the conventions of formal writing. It can serve as a strong and useful adjunct to the *Handbook*. Our best wishes to you as you work on and complete your formal papers utilizing the *Handbook* and this summary of formal writing conventions.

For a quick review of these conventions, refer to the checklist on conventions of formal writing found in Appendix A page 81. The use of the checklist will provide a further review of your paper in terms of formal writing.

End Note

You have now completed a formal paper. This is one of several you will do in your graduate work and in your professional career. The exercise of formal writing is integral to your professional growth and to the development of your professional skills. As you grow professionally you will be expected to communicate your ideas, your perspectives, and your skills through writing as well as through speaking. Much of your written communication will be through formal writing. Formal writing skills help you in organizing, sequencing, interpreting information, drawing conclusions, and making recommendations. The utilization of these skills will be a strong asset in the development of your professionalism. Their use will also provide a basis for your growing perspectives and philosophy about your profession. Every strong leader needs to develop these qualities.

Be sure to keep your formal papers. A collection of these papers can be useful for reference and focus on issues, opportunities, and problems that may be a part of your professional assignment. The references you used for your papers can be a quick guide to obtaining sources and information. The bibliographies you have developed through your papers, particularly those with annotated bibliographies, can be a real asset to you professionally. Keep all of these. Wherever possible organize them topically so you can access sources on a particular issue. As part of your professional development, these papers, the references, and the bibliographies you have collected can be very useful. Professionalism includes keeping current on issues and topics in the field. You should continue to read and reflect on these and add to your bibliography and sources as you continue your personal program of professional development. The acquisition of professional skills and experience can help you achieve you own personal professional goals. Congratulations on completing your paper and on your continuing development as a professional.

References

American Psychological Association. (2001). *Publication manual of the American Psychological Association* (5th ed.). Washington DC: Author.

Bennis, W. G. (1993). *An invented life: Reflections on leadership and change.* New York: Addison-Wesley.

Bennis, W. G. (2000). *Managing the dream.* Cambridge, MA Perseus Books Group.

Bennis, W., & Goldsmith, J. (2003). *Learning to lead* (3rd ed.). Cambridge, MA. Perseus Books Group.

Carver, R. P. (1984). *Writing a publishable research report in education, psychology, and related disciplines.* Springfield, IL: Charles C. Thomas.

Cone, J. D., & Foster, S. L. (1993). *Dissertations and theses from start to finish: Psychology and related fields.* Washington, DC: American Psychological Association.

Darling-Hammond, L (1997). *The right to learn: Blueprint for creating schools that work.* San Francisco, CA: Jossy-Bass Education Series.

Drucker, P. F. (1967). *The effective executive.* New York: Harper and Rowe.

Eisner, E. W. (1994). *The educational imagination on the design and evaluation of school programs.* (3rd ed.). New York: Macmillan College Publishing Company.

Gall, M. D., Borg, W. R., & Borg, J. P. (1996). *Educational research: An introduction* (6th ed.). White Plains, NY: Longman Publishers USA

Howard, R. (Ed.). (1993). *The learning imperative: Managing people for continuous innovation.* Boston, MA: Harvard Business School.

Joyce, B., Weil, M., with Calhoun, E. (2004). *Models of teaching* (7th ed.). Needham Heights, MA:Allyn and Bacon.

Likert, R. (1967). *The human organization.* New York: McGraw Hill.

Merriam, S. B. (1998). *Qualitative research and case study applications in education* (2nd. ed.) San Francisco, CA: Jossey-Bass.

Mertens, D. M. (2004). *Research methods in education and psychology: Integrating diversity with quantitative and qualitative approaches* (2nd ed.). Thousand Oaks, CA: Sage Publishers.

Reeves, D. (2003). *Making standards work* (3rd ed.). Denver. CO: Center for Performance Assessment.

Sample, S. B. (2001). *The contrarian's guide to leadership.* San Francisco, CA: Jossey-Bass.

Steinaker, N. W., & Bell, M. R. (1979). *The experiential taxonomy: A new approach to teaching and learning.* New York: Academic Press.

Turabian, K. L. (1987). *A manual for writers of term papers, theses and dissertations* (5th ed.). Chicago, IL: University of Chicago Press.

Appendix A

Checklists for Sections of Formal Papers and Writing

In the pages that follows are a series of checklists. There is one for every section of the

formal paper you are preparing. Also included are checklists for the table of contents, a

bibliography, and appendixes. A generic checklist for conventions of formal writing in provided.

This checklist for formal writing should be used as the final check of your paper. Each checklist

is designed for your personal review of the paper you have prepared as the writer. You can use

these checklists both as you write and as a final review to determine if you have completed all the

necessary components of each section of your paper or study. This is done to ensure that you

have followed the formal writing conventions as well as the APA format and expected

components of each section of the paper. In addition, if you are a student writer, there is a

signature form for you and for your instructor including the date when the checklist is completed

and provided for the instructor. These checklists can also be used for conferences between you

and your instructor or supervisor. Space is provided on each of the checklists for comments by

you, by your instructor or by your supervisor. Page numbers referents are included to note the

page number in the *Handbook* where the information needed to complete the each point on the

checklist is provided. During the preparation of your paper, you may need to use several of the

checklists more than once when you conference with your instructor or supervisor. If you are

enrolled in a class, these checklists may be provided for you by your instructor. They can also

be obtained through the publisher.

If you are writing your paper individually for submission to a specific audience or to a

journal or other publication, these checklists are provided to ensure that you have followed the

format suggested within the *Handbook* and are consistent with the APA. Be sure to use them

because they provide you with a final check about your adherence to formal writing conventions

and to the format outlined in the *Handbook*.   Again, our best wishes to you as you use these checklists. We are sure that you will find them helpful. If you need additional copies of the checklists or the *Handbook*, please ask your instructor or your supervisor for copies. You may also contact the publisher.

Checklist for Preparing the Title Page

Directions: Please fill out the checklist below. Circle yes or no for each item listed. Make any comments necessary in the space provided. Page numbers following each item indicate the references to the page or pages where you will find the information about how to complete the item.

1. I have included a page header (3)..................................Yes   No

2. I have included a running head (3).................................Yes   No

3. I have provided the full title of my paper (4)........................Yes   No

4. My (our) name (s) as author (s) is listed below the title (4)...................Yes   No

5. I have included the author's affiliation (4)..............................Yes   No

6. I have provided any other information expected by the instructor, the organization,

   or the group to which the paper will be submitted. (3-4) ....Yes   No

7. All elements of the title page are centered as specified and are in place (3-4).......Yes   No

Comments:

_____

_____

_____

_____

Writer's signature_____

Instructor's signature_____

Date_____

Checklist for Table of Contents

Directions: Please fill out the checklist below. Circle yes or no for each item listed. Make any comments necessary in the space provided. Page numbers following each item reference the page or pages on which you will find information necessary to complete the item.

1. Table of contents has a page header numbered in lower case Roman numerals (6). . . Yes   No

2. The table of contents immediately follows the title page (6). . . . . Yes   No

3. Ellipses are correctly entered (6). . . . . Yes   No

4. Section headings or chapter numbers are justified to the left margin (6). . . . . Yes   No

5. Categories are indented one tab space (6). . . . . Yes   No

6. Subcategories are indented two tab spaces (6).. . . . . Yes   No

7. Page numbers are justified to the right margin (6). . . . . Yes   No

8. Appendixes are listed by title and page number in the table of contents (6). . . . . Yes   No

Comments:

_____

_____

_____

_____

Writer's signature_____

Instructor's signature_____

Date_____

Checklist for Preparing the Abstract

Directions: Please fill out the checklist below. Circle yes or no for each item listed. Make any comments necessary in the space provided. Page numbers following each item indicate the reference to the page or pages where you will find the information on how to complete the item.

1. I have included a page header numbered two (3) . . . . .Yes   No

2. The word abstract appears as the title one double space below page header (8). . . . Yes   No

3. My abstract is blocked (8). . . . . Yes   No

4. My abstract contains no more than 120 words (150 if approved by instructor) (8) . Yes   No

5. My abstract is accurate, concise, and specific (9). . . . . Yes   No

6. I have included salient points from the review of literature (9). . . . . .Yes   No

7. The abstract was written in the past tense (9). . . . . Yes   No

8. I have included results of my research study (9). . . . . Yes   No

9. I have included conclusions and recommendations (9). . . . . Yes   No

10. I wrote my abstract after the other sections of the paper were completed (9). . . . . . . Yes   No

11. No personal bias or opinion is included within the abstract (9). . . . . .Yes   No

Comments:

_____

_____

_____

_____

Writer's signature_____

Instructor's signature_____   Date_____

Checklist for Preparing the Introduction

Directions: Please fill out the form below. Circle yes or no for each item listed. Make any comments necessary in the space provided. Page numbers following each item indicate the reference to the page or pages where you will find information on how to complete the item.

1. I have included a page header numbered three (3)............................Yes   No

2. Full title of paper is given one double space below the page header (11)...........Yes   No

3. The purpose of the paper is clearly stated at the beginning of the paper (11).......Yes   No

4. The purpose includes limitations of the topic, the area of study, questions or issues, and other information especially if you are writing a research study (11-12)...........Yes   No

5. The importance of the paper/study has been evidenced with citations (12).........Yes   No

6. Works cited reflected the author's feeling about importance of the topic (12-13).... Yes   No

7. I have prepared my rationale for choosing the topic (13)......................Yes   No

8. Everything in the introduction except from direct quotes was written in the past or present perfect tense (13) .... Yes   No

Comments:

_____

_____

_____

_____

Writer's signature_____

Instructor's signature_____

Date_____

Checklist for Preparing the Review of Literature

Directions: Please fill out the checklist below. Circle yes or no for each item listed. Make any comments necessary in the space provided. Page numbers following each item indicate the reference to the page or pages where you will find the information on how to complete the item.

1. I have included a page header on every page of the review of literature (3). . . . . Yes No

2. Review begins with an opening paragraph listing categories and subcategories (15). . Yes No

3. The categories are on a separate line from text and are italicized (16). . . . . Yes No

4. I have used at least two categories and at least two subcategories where needed (16). .Yes No

5. I have used no personal commentary in any part of the review of literature (16). . . . . Yes No

6. Subcategory names are indented. italicized, followed by a period on a text line (18). . .Yes No

7. I have cited sources for every new idea or information I have introduced (17). . . . . . . Yes No

8. Everything is written in past or present perfect tense except in direct quotes (17). . . . Yes No

9. I have put quotation marks around each quote under forty words along with citation

    and page number (17). . . . . Yes No

10. I have blocked quotes of forty or more words using no quotation marks (17). . . . . . . Yes No

11. I have cited every quote of forty or more words and included page number (17) . . . .Yes No

12. Everything in the review of literature is double spaced.(20). . . . . .Yes No

13. I have provided an evidentiary base for my conclusions and recommendations (20). Yes No

14. If needed, I have included a closing paragraph (18). . . . . Yes No

Comments:

_____

_____

_____

Writer's signature_____   Instructor signature_____   Date_____

Checklist for Preparing the Method Section

Directions: Please fill out the checklist given below. Circle yes or no for each item listed. Make any comments in the space provided. Page numbers following the item are the reference page or pages where you will find information about how to complete the item.

1. I have included a page header for each page (3)............................... Yes   No

2. I have made each of the topics listed as a separate category (21).................. Yes   No

3. I have completed the question or issue section (21-22). . . . . Yes   No

4. I have used the past tense or present perfect tense throughout this section (28)..... Yes   No

5. I have noted limitations, variables, population and sampling process (22-25)........Yes   No

6. I have discussed the time frame and process (25-26)............................ Yes   No

7. I have addressed data collection, data analysis, assessment and evaluation (26-28)... Yes   No

8. I have selected the data analysis mode, either qualitative or quantitative (27-28)..... Yes   No

9. I have provided enough detail in each section for clarity and understanding (28) ..... Yes   No

Comments:

_____

_____

_____

_____

Writer's signature_____

Instructor's signature_____

Date_____

Checklist for Preparing the Results Section

Directions: Please fill out the checklist given below. Circle yes or no for each item listed. Make any comments in the space provided. Numbers following each item are references to the pages in the *Handbook* where you can find information about how to complete each item.

1. I have included a page header on each page of this section (3)................... Yes   No

2. I have obtained results in a quantitative study using descriptive statistics, inferential statistics, or correlational statistical analysis (30-31)*......................... Yes   No

3. I have obtained results in a qualitative study with personal interpretation (33-34))*. Yes   No

4. I have presented my results in a clear and concise way (30-32)................. Yes   No

5. I have included figures or tables, as needed, to present and clarify results (30)...... Yes   No

6. I have written my results section in past or present perfect tense (34)........... Yes   No

7. The results are clearly and cogently written (31-34)......................... Yes   No

8. There is no bias, interpretation, or personal perspective in this section (30)........ Yes   No

9. I have disaggregated the data, as necessary, for each variable in the results (32)...... Yes   No

*   Select only one.

Comments:

_____

_____

_____

_____

Writer's signature_____

Instructor's signature_____Date_____

Checklist for Review of Literature Paper Discussion Section

Directions: Please fill out the checklist given below. Circle yes or no for each item listed. Make any comments in the space provided. Numbers following each item indicate the page numbers in the *Handbook* on which you can find information about how to complete the item.

1. I have included a page header for each page in this section (3). . . . . .Yes No

2. I have included a summary of the review of literature written in past or present perfect

   tense (38). . . . . Yes No

3. I have used citations in the summary (38). . . . . Yes No

4. I have interpreted the literature carefully and clearly using present tense and the

   personal pronoun I (38-39). . . . . Yes No

5. I have provided an evidentiary base for my conclusions (37-38). . . . . Yes No

6. My conclusions are clearly and succinctly stated (39). . . . . Yes No

7. Recommendations are based on evidence, the conclusions, and are clearly stated (39).Yes No

8. I have expressed my personal views on the review of literature in the interpretation, the

   conclusions, and the recommendations. (38-39) . . . . Yes No

9. I did not elaborate or go into detail in my conclusions and recommendations (39). . . .Yes No

Comments:

_____

_____

_____

_____

Writer's signature_____

Instructor's signature_____

Date_____

Checklist for Discussion Section of Research Studies

Directions: Please respond to each item listed below. Circle yes or no for each item. Make any comments in the space provided. Numbers following the item are the reference pages in the *Handbook* on which you can find information about how to complete the item.

1. I have summarized my results and related them to the review of literature (40-41)...Yes   No

2. I have cited studies related to this topic in the summary (40-41))................Yes   No

3. Results of this study have been related to other research studies (40-41)...........Yes   No

4. I have presented my views of results in the interpretation section (41-42)......... Yes   No

5. I have interpreted the review of literature in terms of the results and the content of the

    review of literature (41-42)... Yes   No

6. The review of literature provided an evidentiary base for the study (42)........... Yes   No

7. Conclusions were clear and concise and were drawn from the review of literature and

    the results (42-43)... Yes   No

8. Recommendations were clear and concise and drawn from the review of literature and

    the results (43).. Yes   No

Comments:

_____

_____

_____

_____

Writer's signature_____

Instructor's signature_____

Date_____

Checklist for References Section

Directions: Please respond to each item listed below. Circle yes or no for each item. Make comments in the space provided. Numbers following each item refer to pages in the *Handbook* where you can find information on how to complete the item.

1. References follow the APA style (48). . . . . Yes   No

2. References are alphabetized by author or title when no author is listed (48). . . . . . . Yes   No

3. Internet pathways are listed without underlining and in black with an APA

   approved 12 point typeface (48). . . . . Yes   No

4. Everything in the reference section is double spaced (48). . . . . .Yes   No

5. I have listed only the sources cited in the body of the paper (48). . . . . Yes   No

6. References are hanging reference with succeeding lines indented one tab space (48). . .Yes   No

Comments:

_____

_____

_____

_____

Writer's signature_____

Instructor's signature_____

Date_____

Checklist for Formal Writing

Directions: Please fill out the form below. Circle yes or no for each item listed. Make any comments necessary in the space provided. Page numbers following each item indicate the reference to the page or pages in the *Handbook* where you will find the information about how to complete the item.

1. There are no agreement errors in my paper (51)............................Yes   No

2. I have eliminated all anthropomorphisms from my paper (52)..................Yes   No

3. My citations follow the APA style (52-53)..............................Yes   No

4. I have eliminated colloquialisms, idioms, and slang expressions from my paper (53). Yes   No

5. My ellipses follow *Handbook* guidelines (53).............................Yes   No

6. I have not ended or begun any line in my paper with a hyphen (53).............Yes   No

7. My paper is justified only on the left margin except for page headers (54).........Yes   No

8. I have used specific and precise language in my paper (54)....................Yes   No

9. I have eliminated most or all of the he/shes from my paper (51).................Yes   No

10. I have no comma splices, run on sentences, or fragments in my paper (56-57)......Yes   No

11, I have used that and who correctly (57)..................................Yes   No

12, I have used the appropriate tenses in all sections of my paper (57).............Yes   No

13. There is no plagiarism in my paper (55)................................Yes   No

Comments:

_____

_____

_____

_____

Writer's signature_____   Instructor's signature_____   Date_____

Checklist for Appendixes

Appendixes may not be needed, nor required for your paper or study. If they are, please fill out the checklist below.

Directions: Please fill out the form below. Circle yes or no for each item listed. Make any comments in the space provided. Page numbers following each items are referents for the page or pages on which you will find information needed to complete the item.

1. I have included a page header (3) . . . . Yes   No

2. My appendixes follow the references and the bibliography (if included) (50). . . . . . .Yes   No

3. Each appendix has a title (50). . . . . .Yes   No

4. If more than one appendix is included it is lettered A, B, C, D and so forth (50). . . . Yes   No

5. My appendixes include information pertinent to my paper or study (50). . . . . Yes   No

6. My appendixes are listed in the table of contents (50). . . . . Yes   No

7. I have referred to the appendixes in the appropriate sections of my paper (50). . . . .Yes   No

8. I have followed APA style and format for all appendixes (50). . . . . Yes   No

Comments:

_____

_____

_____

_____

Writer's signature_____

Instructor's signature_____

Date_____

Checklist for Bibliography

A bibliography is not always required in a review of literature or a research study. If it is

required, please complete this checklist.

Directions: Please fill out the form below. Circle yes or no for each item listed. Make any

comments in the space provided. Page numbers following each item are referents for the page or

pages on which you will find information needed to complete the item.

1. I have included a page header for the bibliography (3)..........................Yes   No

2. My bibliography immediately follows the references and is on a separate page (50) Yes   No

3. My bibliography contains only additional resources directly related to my topic(50) Yes   No

4. I have annotated each entry in the bibliography (50)........................... Yes   No

5. My annotations are blocked and begin one double space below the entry (50).......Yes   No

6. I have followed APA for each entry into the bibliography (50)................... Yes   No

7. Entries are listed by author or title where no author is given (50)................Yes   No

8. I have not included entries unrelated to the topic of my paper (50).............. Yes   No

Comments

_____

_____

_____

_____

Writer's signature_____

Instructor's signature_____

Date_____

Appendix B

Suggested Scoring Rubrics

Below is a suggested scoring rubric for review of literature papers and research papers. You may make any adjustments needed for your class or for your course. The first scoring rubric is for review of literature papers, the second is for research studies. These rubrics are based on a hundred point scale.

Review of Literature Papers

Adherence to APA style as noted in the *Handbook*. 15

Follows conventions of formal writing and writing tips in the *Handbook*. 10

Content of the introduction. 5

Content of the review of literature. 55

Content of the discussion. 10

References. 5

Research Studies

Adherence to APA style as noted in the *Handbook*. 15

Follows conventions of formal writing and writing tips in the *Handbook*. 10

Content of introduction. 10

Content of review of literature. 15

Content of method section. 15

Content of results section. 15

Content of discussion. 10

References. 10

Appendix C

Suggested Evaluation Guide

Below are suggested evaluation deductions from papers. You can use this or one of your own construction. Any changes you wish to make can be used for your class. The numbers indicate the suggested loss of points. If the number is two or more you can deduct up to that number.

1. Major syntax error (comma fault, run on, fragment). 3

2. Failure to follow APA format as found in *Handbook*. 5

3. More than three agreement errors. 1

4. Organization of paper. 4

5. Reference errors. 1

6. Errors in citations. 1

7. Errors in quotations (block quotations, direct quotes, page numbers). 1

8. Errors in tense (consistent use of wrong tense). 3

9. Referent errors. 1

10. Spacing errors (everything is double spaced). 2

11. Errors in table of contents (where required). 1

12. Errors in abstract (number of words, not blocked, missing some elements). 1

13. Word choice (use precise word). 1

14. Sentences (mostly simple sentences; some compound or complex sentences). 2

15. Use of superscript or subscript except in certain mathematics or science formulae. 1

16. Errors in ellipses. 1

17. Other errors (to be determined by instructor). 2

Appendix D

Format for Presentation of Paper

This format is designed for oral presentations. Power Point presentations can be used in conjunction with oral presentations. Other media may also be used. Organization is key to a strong presentation. As Pope noted "brevity is the soul of wit." Do not be loquacious or verbose. As we have already stated, verbosity is the last refuge of mediocrity. We have keyed this presentation format to a brief presentation of five to eight minutes with two minutes for questions and comments. Longer presentations can go into greater detail and more specificity. They will take more time, but should follow the same format presented below. The presentation format is consistent with the organization of the paper.

Review of Literature Paper

1. State the purpose of your paper.

2. Establish the importance of the topic. This can be done in one or two sentences.

3. Note why you chose this topic.

4. Identify the categories and subcategories of the review of literature.

5. Highlight one or two salient points from each category.

6. In the discussion summarize your review of literature.

7. In the discussion Interpret your review of literature.

8. Cite your conclusions.

9. Make your recommendations

This is all you do for a review of literature paper. For brief presentations, this kind of oral presentation can be done in five minutes or less. Longer presentations, if agreed upon by the instructor or supervisor, can be made.

Research Studies

1. State the purpose of your study. Include information about area of study, limitations, variables, and other pertinent information. State these briefly.

2. Establish the importance of your topic. Use citations as needed.

3. Tell why you selected the topic

4. Name the categories and subcategories of the review of literature.

5. Identify salient points from the review of literature including other studies about the topic.

6. For the method section restate the purpose of the study, mention time frame, limitations, population, sampling, process, data collection, data analysis, and assessment and evaluation. Do this briefly and avoid any redundancies. Sometimes you can bring two or more categories of the method section together. Tailor the details to the allotted time frame for presentation.

7. Present the results section by noting the variables tested, the and the statistical measures used for analysis.

8. Provide result for each variable keyed to statements on surveys, questionnaires, and interviews.

9. Note the ones on which you are reporting and give results for each.

10. Inferential and correlational statistical analyses require statements of significance.

11. Note any comments from surveys or questionnaires

12. Establish the meaning of the results in a summative statement.

13. Summarize the review of literature and emphasize how it related to your study.

14. Correlate your findings with the review of literature.

15. Interpret the meaning of your findings including interpretation of the literature reviewed.

16. State your conclusions.

17. State your recommendations.

With careful organization and the presentation of only the most important information, a brief report of this kind can be completed in five to eight minutes with a few minutes for questions an comments following. Any presentation should be tightly organized, succinctly presented, as well as being clear and cogent to the audience. Longer presentations can, of course be allowed by the instructor or supervisor. Best wishes to you on your presentation.

Appendix E

Sample References

Below are listed some references most of which are taken directly from the APA manual. Review these and if you have additional questions, please ask your instructor or supervisor or refer directly to the APA manual.

Book, two authors

Steinaker, N. W., & Bell, M. R. (1979). *The experiential taxonomy: A new approach to teaching and learning.* New York: Academic Press.

Journal article, three to six authors

Saywitz, K. J., Mannarino, A. P., Berliner, L., & Cohen, J. A. (2000). Treatment for sexually abused children and adolescents. *American Psychologist*, 55, 1040-1049.

Magazine article

Kandel, E. R., & Squire, L. R. (2000, November 10), Neuroscience: Breaking down scientific barriers to the study of brain and mind. *Science*, 290, 1112-1120.

Daily newspaper article, no author

New drug appears to sharply cut risk of death from heart failure. (1993, July 15). *The Washington Post*, p. A12.

Abstract as original source

Wood, N. J., Young, S. L., Fanselow, M. S. & Butcher, L. L. (1991). MAP-2 expression in cholinoceptive pyramidal cells or rodent cortex and hippocampus is altered by Pavlovian conditioning [abstract]. *Society for Neuroscience Abstracts*. 17, 480.

Book, third edition, Jr. in name

Mitchell, T. R., & Larson, J. R., Jr. (1987). *People in organizations: An introduction to organizational behavior* (3rd ed.). New York: McGraw-Hill.

Edited book

Gibbs, J. T., & Huang, L. N. (Eds.), (1991). *Children of color: Psychological interventions with*

   minority youth. San Francisco: Jossey-Bass.

Article or chapter from an edited book, two editors

Bjork, R. A. (1989). Retrieval inhibition as an adaptive mechanism in human memory. In H. L.

   Roediger II & F. I. M. Craik (Eds.), *Varieties of memory & consciousness* (pp. 309-330).

   Hillsdale, NJ: Erlbaum.

Entry in an encyclopedia

Bergmann, P. G. (1993). Relativity. In *The new encyclopaedia Britannica* (Vol. 26, pp. 501-558).

   Chicago: Encyclopaedia Britannica.

Note: When the article has no author listed, place the title in the author position.

Report available from ERIC

Mead, J. V. (1992). *Looking at old photographs: Investigating the teacher tales that novice*

   teachers bring with them (Report No. NCRTL-RR-9204). East Lansing, MI: National

   Center for Research on Teacher Learning. (ERIC Document Reproduction Service

   No. ED346082).

Published proceedings of meetings or symposia

Deci, E. L., & Ryan, R. M. (1991). A motivational approach to self: Integration in personality.

   In R. Dienstbier (Ed.). *Nebraska Symposium on Motivation:* Vol. 38. *Perspectives on*

   motivation (pp. 237-288). Lincoln: University of Nebraska Press.

Doctoral dissertations and master's theses abstracted in *Dissertation Abstracts*

International **from the University of Michigan**

Brower, D. L. (1993). Employee assistant programs supervisory referrals: Characteristics of

   referring and nonreferring supervisors. *Dissertation Abstracts International, 54* (01),

534B. (UMI No. 9315947)

Unpublished manuscript not submitted for publication

Stinson, C., Milbrath, C, Reidbord, S. & Bucci, W. (1992). *Thematic segmentation of*

psychotherapy transcripts for convergent analyses. Unpublished manuscript.

Manuscript in progress or submitted for publication but not yet accepted

Steinaker, N. W., Mbuva, J, & Holm, M. (2005). *A taxonomy of motivation: From theory to*

practice. Manuscript submitted for publication.

Internet articles based on a print source

VandenBos, G., Knapp, S., & Doe, J. (2001). Role of reference elements in the selection of

resources by psychology undergraduates [Electronic version], *Journal of Bibliographic*

Research, 5, 117-123.

Stand-alone internet document, no author identified, no date

GVU's 8th WWW user survey. (n.d.). Retrieved August 8, 2000, from

http://www.cc.gatech.edu/gvu/user_surveys/survey-1997-10/

Message posted to a newsgroup

Chalmers, D. (2000, November 17). Seeing with sound [Msg 1]. Message posted to

news://sci.psychology.consciousness

Electronic copy of a journal article, retrieved from database

Borman, W. C., Hanson, M. A., Oppler, S. H., Pulakos, E. D., & White, L. A. (1993). Role of

early supervisor performance. *Journal of Applied Psychology,* 78, 443-449. Retrieved

October 23, 2000, from PsychARTICLES database.

Appendix F

Preparing Surveys and Questionnaires

Often in preparation for a research study you need to prepare a survey or a questionnaire. Both need to begin with a strong focus on the purpose of your study. Develop a simple and direct set of directions for filling out the survey or questionnaire. Start your survey or questionnaire with demographic questions about the population you are asking to respond to your survey or your questionnaire. Demographic information includes such elements as age, gender, work assignment, ethnicity, area of residence, and other descriptive demographic information. Demographic information is important because from this information you may identify some or all of the variables you wish to test.

Next you develop statements or questions to gather responses from your population. Determine the most important information you want to obtain and include those statements or questions early in the survey or questionnaire. Make statements or ask questions that are clearly written and can be easily understood by your population. Avoid value words wherever possible and avoid words that can be interpreted in more than one way. Make your statements and questions specific, to the point, and limited to identified information you wish to obtain. Make sure that each question or statement addresses only one issue or area about which to respond. In a survey make space available to comments by respondents. If you wish to have them respond to a specific statement, make space available after that statement. You may also make space available at the end of the survey. In a questionnaire establish some limits to your questions. You may want to ask your respondents to use only the space provided. You may also want to get as much information as possible, so invite them to extend their responses if they wish.

If you are using a survey, you may use a Likert Scale which has strongly agree, agree, disagree, strongly disagree possible responses. You may use a numeric scale and ask your

population to circle the number that describes their response. Make sure you identify what each number means. You may also use a semantic differential scale if you wish. There are a variety of formats for your survey. Select the one that best fits the population you are studying.

You may also use any of these formats for a questionnaire if you wish. Many questionnaires are set up for comments as responses;. In a survey or questionnaire you can tally your responses and then use statistical measure and to analyze, assess, and interpret them. You can summarize or categorize the comments. You may also wish to identify the responses; through the demographic data you have collected. Make sure as you develop your instrument that it can serve to elicit responses that will help you gather the data you need to find results that focus on the major purpose of your study.

Glossary of Terms

In this glossary of terms are entries, many of which you will use in your review of literature or in your research study. Others are included that you may need as you review literature and other studies related to your paper or research study.

Analysis of covariance (ANCOVA). A procedure for determining whether the difference between the mean scores of two or more groups on one or more dependent variables is statistically significant.

Anecdotal record. A record of behaviors or activities that occur at designated times or when the behaviors or activities occur.

Aptitude test. A measure of abilities that are assumed to be relevant to performance on an identified type of skill or area of achievement.

Artifacts. Objects created by members of past or present cultures.

Baseline. In single case studies the natural behavior patterns of the subject of the study.

Bias. Personal and unreasonable distortion of judgment in such a way that certain facts are habitually overlooked, distorted, or falsified.

Case study research. Study of a phenomenon in its natural context from the perspective of the participants.

Category. In the review of literature a major component of the review. There must be at least two in the review of literature. A component of frequency count data.

Chain of evidence. In qualitative research the validation of the study's findings by clear meaningful links in terms of the study's questions, the raw data analysis and findings.

Chi square. An inferential test of statistical significance used when research data are in the form of frequency counts in two or more categories.

Citation. Information about a document or resource that one would need in order to locate it. A

citation contains the name of the author and the year of publication. It is in parantheses

following the quotation or paraphrase. If no author is listed use the first two words of the title.

Cognitive taxonomy. A classification of cognition developed by Bloom and colleagues.

Initially the taxonomy had six categories. This was revised to seven including: Memory,

translation, interpretation, application, analysis, synthesis, and evaluation.

Correlational research. An investigation that seeks to discover the direction and magnitude of

the relationships between two or more variables through the use of correlational statistics.

Dependent variable. The variable the researcher is interested in measuring to determine how it

is different for groups with different experience or characteristics.

Descriptor. A term or used to classify information about the topic in the classification of

documents or to describe briefly categories of information.

Descriptive statistics. Statistical analyses which describe the data collected. They include

mean, median, mode, range, and standard deviation. In qualitative research, investigation that

involves providing a detailed portrayal of one or more cases.

Diagnostic test. A test used to determine a student's strengths and weaknesses in a particular

subject.

Disaggregated data. Data reported in the results section on identified groups within the

population tested.

Educational Resources Information Center (ERIC). A federally funded agency that provides

information resources to the education community.

Emergent design. In qualitative studies, the practice of changing the design of the study or

evaluation as the evaluator or researcher gains new insights into the concerns and issues of the

group being studied.

Emic perspective. Research participants perceptions of their social reality.

Epistemology. The study of the nature of knowledge

.Experiential taxonomy. A *gestalt* taxonomy developed by Steinaker & Bell that incorporates the cognitive and affective taxonomies in a five step sequence that can be used for teaching and evaluating student work.

Ethnography. The in depth study of life in an identified culture and patterns within it. The focus is on society and culture. Ethnographic studies uncover and describe beliefs, values, and attitudes of a group.

Etic perspective. The researcher's perspective of the research participants social reality.

Experimenter bias. A situation in which the experimenter or author's expectations about what will occur are transmitted to the research participants behavior in the study is affected. Also a situation in which the researcher's expectations affect data collection and data analysis.

Extinction. The practice of behavior modification through the withdrawal of an intervention in behavioral research.

Formative evaluation. Evaluation of the process of a study done while the program is underway.

Generalizability. Researcher's ability to generalize results from the sample from which it was drawn and relate those generalizations to transferability.

Grounded theory. An approach to theory development in qualitative research. Grounded theory emerges from the data collected and the narrative associated with those data. It is an emergent theory and does not depend on an existing theory.

Hermeneutics. A field of inquiry that seeks to understand how individuals develop interpretations and consensus about issues and tasks.

Historical research. A study of past phenomena for the purpose of gaining a better understanding of present institutions, practices, trends, and issues.

Hypothesis. A researcher's prediction, derived from theory or from speculation, about how two or more variables will be related to each other.

Independent variable. The treatment or intervention the researcher uses with the experimental group in an experimental design within quantitative research.

Inferential statistics. Statistical protocols designed to determine significance.

Institutional review board (IRB). A committee established by an institution to ensure that participants in research projects will be protected from harm. The IRB reviews and approves research done by members of the institution.

Inter rater reliability. A measure to determine if two or more raters reliably measure criteria with similar standards and results.

Interval recording. The recording of observational behaviors at given time intervals.

Item analysis. A set of procedures for determining the difficulty, the reliability, and the validity of each item on a test.

Likert scale. A measure that asks individuals to check their level of agreement with various statements.

Longitudinal research. An investigation that involves describing changes in a sample's characteristics over a specified period of time.

Matrix. In a qualitative research report, a type of table that has defined rows and columns for reporting the results of data analyses and other information.

Mean. A measure of central tendency calculated by the sum of the score in a set by the numbers of scores.

Median. A measure of central tendency corresponding to the middle score in a range of scores.

Meta analysis. Statistical procedures to identify trends from the results of a set of studies on the same problem or issue.

Mode. A measure of central tendency corresponding to the most frequently occurring score in a distribution of scores.

Multiple regression. A statistical procedure for determining the relationship between a criterion variable and a combination of two or more predictor variables.

NCE score. A type of scoring with a mean of 50. The scores are continuous and have an equality of units. There are 100 scores in all and they correspond to individual percentages.

Normal curve. A distribution of scores that form a symmetrical, bell shaped curve when plotted on a graph.

Objectivity. The extent to which the narrative or the scores on a test by the biases of the researcher or the writer.

Ontology. The study of the nature of reality.

Ordinal scale. A measure in which numbers represent a rank ordering of individuals or objects on some variable.

Outlier. A research participant's score on a measure which differs markedly from other scores.

Parameter. The boundary of a study, a series of scores, or the characteristics of a population's scores.

Paraphragiarism. Borrowing of another author's writing to such an extent as to constitute the representation of the other author's work as your own. Similar to plagiarism.

Pattern. In qualitative research instances in which certain behaviors, attitudes, or actions are systematically related to each other.

Pearson r. In correlational statistical analysis a mathematical expression of the direction and magnitude of the relationship between two measures with continuous scores.

Percentile. A type of rank score that represents a raw score as the percentage of individuals in the norming group whose scores fall below that score.

Pilot study. A small scale preliminary investigation conducted to develop and test the measures used in a research study.

Positivism. An epistemological belief that reality is independent of those who observe it, and that observations of this reality, if unbiased, constitute scientific knowledge.

Postmodernism. A broad social and philosophical movement that questions the rationality of human action, the use of positivist epistemology, and any human endeavor that claims a privileged position with respect to the search for truth.

Posttest. A measure that is administered following an experimental or control treatment in order to determine the effects of the intervention. A posttest only is a test given to both experimental and control groups following the intervention with the experimental group.

Presentism. Interpreting past events in terms of concepts and perspectives that originated in recent times.

Pretest. A measure administered prior to an experimental treatment or other intervention.

Qualitative research. Inquiry that is grounded in the assumption that individuals construct social reality in the form of meaning and interpretations, and that these constructions tend to be transitory and situational.

Quantitative research. Inquiry that is grounded in the assumption that features of the social environment constitute and objective reality that is relatively constant across time and settings.

Random assignment. The process of assigning individuals or groups to the experimental or control treatment in order that each individual or group has an equal chance of being in each group.

Range. The difference between the highest and the lowest scores in a distribution.

Reliability. The extent to which a test yields the same or similar results in repeated administration.

Rubric. A scale to measure different levels of proficiency demonstrated by students.

Sampling. The process of selecting members of a research sample from a defined population.

Semantic differential scale. A measure that asks individuals to rate an attitude on a series of bipolar adjective (fair-unfair, valuable-worthless, hot-cold).

Semiotics. The study of sign systems. In particular the study of how objects come to meaning and how sign systems affect human behavior.

Snowball sampling. Cases that are selected by asking one person to recommend others with similar experiences.

Standard deviation. A measure of the extent that scores in a distribution deviate from their mean.

Statistic. Any number that describes a characteristic of a sample's score on a measure.

***t* Score.** A probability distribution used to determine level of statistical significance of an obtained *t* value of the difference between two sample means.

Test. A structured performance situation that can be analyzed to yield numerical scores.

Theory. An explanation of the commonalities and the relationships among observed phenomena in terms of causual structure and processes that are presumed to underlie them.

Triangulation. The use of multiple data collection methods, data sources, analysts, or theories a corroborative evidence for the validity of qualitative research findings.

Validity. Measures which determine if the test or measure for data collection is consistent with the content of what is being tested.

Variable. A characteristic of the sample of the population. Data from the characteristic are collected, analyzed and reported.